# Tro-tros
# and Potholes

## West Africa: Solo

*To Colleen,*
*Enjoy all your travels*
*Laura*

By Laura Enridge

**Tro-tros and Potholes**
**West Africa: Solo**

Cover design by Jon Winebrenner
Photos taken by Laura Enridge
Book design by Tracey Martinsen

 Published by Four Corners Publishing, Vancouver
http://www.fourcornerspublishing.com

ISBN 0-9733534-0-6

First edition July 2003
Printed in Canada

# Preface

I was one of the recipients of Laura's e-mails. I lived in hope of receiving an e-mail each day, although I knew that it would be difficult finding an Internet café in the remote areas of Africa where Laura would naturally be. However, she did it. She kept in touch. I read each e-mail and then read it again. And again.

I lived vicariously through these stories and felt as though I was with Laura at each step of the journey. I had a great trip in my armchair imagination. In fact, I was so inspired by the stories, I wanted to make a collection for Laura.

That activity developed into this book.

Heather Duncan
Friend and collaborator on this work,
Vancouver, B.C.

# Acknowledgments

Very special are those who have extended their support, assistance and friendship to me on this project.

I'd like to take this opportunity to mention the following people and express my gratitude for their contributions: Marion Bonner, Andrew, Matt & Julie Dixon, Malcolm & Jean Duncan, Richard Duncan, Andrea Dyck, Norman & Riitta Enridge, Roy Heaton, Julia Kozak, Tracey Martinsen, Catherine Meleady, Neal Parker, Jon Steeves, Scott Thibodeau, Jon Winebrenner, the Johannesburg Four (Elaine, Feyrouz, Kendall and Paisley), and Francis Zera.

I'd also like to thank Heather Duncan for her vision and determination, which eventually became mine, too.

# Dedication

To Fred, the high-school history teacher who gave me my first glimpses into the richness of the world that is out there, and to my friend and surrogate mother Bootzy, who showed me what a safe place it can really be.

# Table of Contents

**Tro-tros and Potholes**

# Prologue

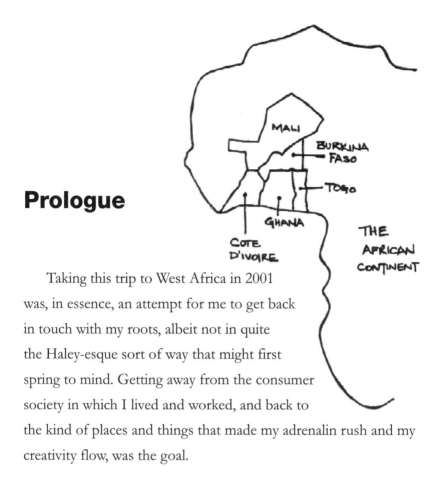

Taking this trip to West Africa in 2001 was, in essence, an attempt for me to get back in touch with my roots, albeit not in quite the Haley-esque sort of way that might first spring to mind. Getting away from the consumer society in which I lived and worked, and back to the kind of places and things that made my adrenalin rush and my creativity flow, was the goal.

Traditionally, the places that have provided the greatest respite for me are those least travelled by other tourists. That's not to say that I don't like beach resorts, I just like beach resorts of the type where you might happen upon another person, and you might not; where the fanciest, most done-up restaurant is the thatched-roof place that gives you paper napkins so you don't have to wipe your hands on your shorts. North America and Europe, I think, have seen enough of me for a while. I've sampled parts of the Middle East, Australia, Southeast Asia, and Central and South America, and definitely want to go back for more. The continent that has topped my list, though, in terms of "getting away from it all," is Africa. From there, I can't seem to stay away.

One of my greatest passions is international development. I love learning about it, working in it, observing and debating it. The political systems that go hand in hand with it are also a fascination. My interest first reached a peak in 1993—94, when I spent a year on the African continent, working my way from east to south. For six months of that time, I was doing a volunteer internship in community development. Although arranged by an American non-profit organization in Washington, D.C., I was on the staff of a local Johannesburg non-profit called the Grasmere Community Development Trust. Our work was centered on three squatter camps that had sprung up outside of the Gold City — row upon row and mile after mile of families in shacks, with no immediate access to running water, medical care, or other such basic amenities. The work was very humbling. Amazingly enough, my connections within the non-profit sector in Johannesburg also afforded me the opportunity to act as an official electoral commission observer in the elections that brought Nelson Mandela to power. It was the kind of experience that I'm quite sure only happens once in a lifetime.

My return home, and the next phase of my life, did little to influence me otherwise. I began feeling like my life had become rather anti-climactic. I worked for six years in the technology sector, learning a great deal of valuable knowledge, but feeling largely uninspired. The grassroots girl in a suit could hold her own with the best of the corporate crowd, but it sure was a monochrome existence. Already unhappy in the job I was holding at the time, I decided to walk away, and got onto a plane bound for Accra (by way of London and Johannesburg, to visit some dear friends along the way). My departure date was March 30, 2001, and with mortgage payments covered through August and my dog Ozwald neatly loaned out to my parents, I set off for three-and-a-half months of wonderful exploration.

The countries that I visited — Ghana, Côte d'Ivoire, Mali, Burkina Faso, and Togo — were among the most fantastic studies of contrast of any place I'd ever been. They were both ancient and modern, deferent and bold, corrupt and virtuous. And four out of five of them were French-speaking. By going there, not only was I repeatedly placing myself in surroundings that were completely outside the boundaries of my comfort zone, I was at the disadvantage of being restricted in my communication. It proved to be a very difficult aspect of the trip. I believe, though, that it left me with a great deal of opportunity to just stay inside my own head, reflecting on what I saw and heard, as opposed to rushing from event to event in the speediness of the spoken word.

This trip was also the first time in 15 years of traveling that I'd made serious use of e-mail as an accompaniment to my journal writing. In a region of the world where other backpackers were few and sometimes far between, it was an important link for me to have. It preserved my sanity by allowing me to vent, and, at the same time, gave me an opportunity to express to my friends and family some of my experiences as they happened.

Now, two years later, you are about to read these occasionally frantic and often self-indulgent communications, uncut and unedited, intermingled with a dozen or so stories that were written after my return home. The e-mails, which start out this book, can be distinguished from the stories by the date and location that follows the title (and sometimes by the poor grammatical constuction!).

I hope that together, they provide a humorous window into that crazy, magical part of the world I dropped in on. It's a magic that I'd like to share, and I'm grateful for being able to do so.

Laura Enridge
Vancouver, 2003

# Chapter 1
# Ditches Deep, Rastas High

**20 April 2001: Accra, Ghana**

Hey all! This is just a quick note now that I have arrived in Ghana. Got into Accra on Wed night after a splendid time in Jo'burg, although ran out of time there and didn't get to see everybody or do everything that I wanted to. Postscript on S.A. for Elaine, Pais, Kendall & Rouz — did we ever actually figure out what is in Monkey Gland sauce?

Accra is a bustling city, lots of traffic, lots of shops and restaurants, quite built up really. And seems to be thriving too. I'm having a good time cruising around. Must watch that I don't fall in the ditches though. All along the streets there are these one to three-foot deep drainage ditches and one small slip and it's all over! I'm having a good laugh over all the hilarious signs everywhere. One good one was "The Millennium Bridge, Constructed by the Handyman for this Electoral Area, Nov. 2000, For the Glory of God." Basically, it was just a two-foot long crossing over one of the ditches, but hey, I guess it meant a lot to somebody. Even with all the traffic there are still a lot of goats and chickens running around, and I have once again gotten used to being woken by a rooster in the early hours.

I'm heading off just now to go fetch my passport at the Ivory Coast embassy and then I'm going to the craft market and the National Museum. Haven't met anybody yet in these two days to hang out with, but then the place I'm staying doesn't really have a good courtyard or any-thing — imperative if you want to meet up with folks. Although I did get an interesting invitation from a Rasta-farian guy when I was sitting in a restaurant area yester-day. He was a funny one. Tomorrow I'll be off to Kokrobite, a beach village about 60 km west of here, where I can also take drum lessons, so I shall be sitting under the palm trees and bongo-ing away. Lovely. After that I shall be working my way west some more, then north a bit, then west again. How's that for a plan?!

Any news on the Canucks and their playoff games would be greatly appreciated. Missing you guys, can't believe it's already been three weeks since I've been gone.

All the best,
Love Laura xox

# Chapter 2
# No Solution is a Problem

---

## 21 April 2001: Accra, Ghana

Okay I had to write again and vent. I didn't leave Accra today because I never made it to the National Museum yesterday (spent too long in the Arts Centre at all the craft stalls trying to figure out how much stuff I can get on the plane or how I can ship it all home when I come back through Accra in July). So I stayed an extra day to do that, and also to source out some contact solution.

The day started out pretty good, except that it was hot hot hot and as I walked to the museum my sweaty feet were rubbing around in my sandals so I got mondo blisters. So that made me not so happy. But when I got to the museum, I enjoyed the display and I also got adopted by a group of seven or eight sweet little children between the ages of seven and ten (I asked them). They couldn't read very well so they wanted me to show them around, which I did because they were sweet and cute and eager to learn — I mean, hey, they'd walked to the Museum all by themselves on a Saturday, no less! But anyway, there was a special exhibit on slavery so we were talking about that and boy did they know a lot about slavery for a bunch of young'uns. I was happy that Canada wasn't in on that whole deal otherwise I would've felt like a schmuck. But a couple of Danish guys were there who did feel like schmucks because the Danes were singled out in one particular case exhibit. So eventually off they went (to another museum, can you believe it?) and I finished up and then began my search for contact solution.

Well apparently no one in Ghana wears lenses because I couldn't find anything to save my life. I took a taxi to the main shopping district because I couldn't walk anymore due to blisters and was then absolutely assaulted by throngs of bodies and chickens and cars and fish and more fish and fish everywhere (didn't smell so nice). Went into at least 10 pharmacies. Nothing. Now in Nairobi once I did a homemade solution by mixing 20 volume hydrogen peroxide with distilled water but nobody even had distilled water!!! So I was stuck. Then I caught a guy with his hand on the zipper of my pack, and in the particularly bad mood that I was I told him I'd kill him if he tried that. So he made haste. Finally I found a hawker that was selling thongs, which made my feet much happier to have all my toes exposed and free again.

I was told by a couple of people to try the pharmacy at the hospital, so I even took a cab there and waited in a huge line (because power was out so they had to do everything by hand and it was taking a long long time) but still no luck. I sat outside the hospital on the stairs for about a half an hour just feeling miserable and hot and completely stymied. Oh April, I wish I'd gone in with you and gotten the damn laser surgery done! Next time for sure, I'm telling you! So now I face the prospect of being in hot and sweaty Africa and having to wear my glasses all day. Ugh. Next town I hit I'm going to look for an optician or something and try that route.

Anyway, to console myself I went to this sports bar called Champs that is run by a Canadian guy and had a big greasy hamburger and fries and a beer and was hoping to see some hockey but it's not on til Sunday night (he has satellite) so I ended up watching stupid cricket instead (sorry Sheila and Jill). And then to find out from e-mails that the Nucks were out in four straight! Ah, my heart is broken.

April, your e-mail about honking horns in Kathmandu is so right on because the very same thing is driving me crazy here. There are like 50 million taxis on the road and they all honk at me when they go past, or yell out the window "Whereyougoing?" So people don't just honk here, they honk AT YOU!! But I have luckily not fallen in any holes yet, so I'm up on you in that respect!

Okay well I'm glad I've had my little vent, I feel much better. I'm going to go back to the guesthouse and crash so I can make an early start for Kokrobite tomorrow morning. As I was leaving some English guys were coming in who said they hadn't slept for four days because they'd been in the Volta region. Wonder what happened there? Oh, Dad, here's the closest thing I can give you to contact names/places — I'm going to be in Kokrobite, then Cape Coast/Elmina, then Kumasi, then Takoradi, then on to Ivory Coast to Abidjan on May 6th.

'kay everybody. Other than being hot and not finding contact solution (how can something that simple be SO DIFFICULT) I am just fine, well, except sunburnt on my back in the pattern of my daypack straps, but then hey its better than sunglass-face-tan lines.

Bye for now!
Laura xoxox

# Chapter 3
# Tro-tros and Potholes

## 1 May 2001: Kumasi, Ghana

Hey everybody! How are things in Vancouver and other parts of the world? I've been gone over a month now, time is a flying! And I've only had the shits twice so far!

I am now in Kumasi, in Ghana. I LOVE GHANA! It is so fun. I think I might come back in for a bit in July and hang out before I come home, especially if I get tired of trying to speak French in all those other places that I'm going.

Anyway, I spent five nights in Kokrobite, what a cool place. There were a bunch of British VSOs there on their Easter break because most of them are teachers in the north here, so we had plenty of fun nights sitting under the palm trees, one or two of the guys playing guitar, just sitting back. I also zipped through two great books in Kokro — I LOVE that I have time to read! Anyway, must recommend Barney's Version by Mordechai Richler.

Excellent. Had a drum lesson there which was also très cool, except that I don't have the stubby calloused hands that my teacher had. He's played in London, Innsbruck and Singapore and is part of a drumming and dancing troupe and he was just excellent. Can't wait to sit on my patio at home with my big ass drum and annoy my neighbours.

Cape Coast was a bit of a let down as a town overall. The only sit-down restaurant was the one attached to the Mobil gas station at the edge of town, so I ate there twice in one day and just had bananas and peanuts the day before that! I'm not too keen on the local food. The main dish is fufu and it really is exactly that. Crappy. All the main dishes are made of a staple based from either yams or plantains or maize and bashed into a gummy, solid consistency, sometimes fermented, then splathered with an oily sauce with fish and stuff in it. So I'm sticking to the basics of bread and rice wherever possible, but still getting waaay too much starch in my diet.

The Cape Coast castle was very interesting — old slave trading fort — so all of that history really hits home when you're standing in a dark, stinky, sweltering hot slave dungeon and imagining what it was like having 1500 people packed in there. Horrific.

The place I stayed at was pretty noisy as there was church stuff going on all the time, day and night. And a disco or two closeby too, I'm quite sure. But man do they have a lot of funerals here. I used to think that there was a disproportionately large number of chair rental places in Ghana, but that's because anywhere there's space, they throw up some chairs and have a service.

Spent two nights in the Boabeng-Fiema Monkey Sanctuary, which was superb. Had a walk in the forest with a park ranger and fed the monkeys some mangoes. Oh how I love primates. Actually I met a woman there who is doing her doctoral research there as a primatologist for the University of Calgary, a Jane Goodall of sorts but far more normal, so I've been hanging out with her for a couple of days and we came into Kumasi together today as she needed to get out of the bush for a break. It is really quite out of the way. On my trip there it was pouring rain and the roads were just mudpits, so a logging truck got stuck diagonally across the road, blocking it, and my transport had to turn back, so me and a villager that was sharing the car with me had to walk the last two or three kms in the rain, me with all my gear, trying hard not to slip and fall down in the mud. Aaaahh, this is Africa. At least it was still light out.

I'll be leaving Kumasi on the 3rd, I believe, heading for either Takoradi or Elmina or Busua. Or maybe Dixcove. It's a cunning plan!

I've taken the advice of the Peace Corp and VSO people who have all said don't travel on the tro-tros at night because they just smack into each other all over the roads. I can believe it, they are atrocious drivers. A successful tro-tro journey is measured by how many times I bite my tongue when we suddenly WHOMP go over a pothole. Oh, and by not crashing, too, of course.

On today's lift the woman beside me decided to squish her two children in as well in the space that was intended just as her seat, but she was kind enough to remove her babies shoes so that I just had bare toes jamming into the back of my knee for three hours instead.

The kids have a bad habit here of wanting to touch me, which usually doesn't bother me except the other day when this three year old was whizzing into a ditch, dribbling all over his hands, and then he came running at me, arms outstretched. I did a bob and weave and got away. Oh, and some kids have also told me I have a big nose. "Why yes," I said, "I guess I do have a big nose compared to yours!"

All in all, Africa is grand. Hope you are all well and healthy and eating less starch than me. Mmmm I miss salads.....

Laura xoxoxo

# Chapter 4
# A Coastline of Fortresses

I have a vague recollection of cranking out a history term paper about the African slave trade in second-year university (writing papers at the rate of one a week does not generally lend itself to good memory retention of their content). I think that I regurgitated some statistics on the number of people that were taken from Africa, the routes that they travelled, and the horrific conditions on the ships that sometimes killed half of the unwilling passengers before they even reached their destination. What I do remember is that I only got a C- on the paper. It seems my professor, bless his hard-assed soul (I was otherwise getting As in political science) may have felt that my comprehension and analysis of the social impact of this era had shown some limits.

Fifteen years later, I'll concede that that much may have been true. I've always felt that you can't truly understand the historical depths and dimensions of a place until you visit it, hence my eagerness to go everywhere. And until my arrival in Ghana, I hadn't experienced anything that could bridge the gap between all of my book-learning and the true extent of the visible scars that the slave trade had left behind.

At its height in the eighteenth century, a slave fort had marked the shoreline every six kilometres. It was an era when Ghana was known as the Gold Coast, but the memories that the sight of these still-numerous forts evoke are definitely not golden.

Slave forts are the foundation of almost 200 years of the capture and deportation of tens of thousands of people from countries all along the west coast of Africa. They spring up in town after town, formidable, misleadingly-beautiful and almost castle-like. They stand as landmarks in practically every town that allowed access to the open seas, bigger, stronger and exuding more power than any buildings constructed there today. For Ghanaians, to live in their midst is a constant reminder of an era when the families of their ancestors were split apart without a moment's warning, shipped away to an unknown destination and an even lesser-known fate.

What kind of impact must such a legacy have on a nation? I wondered. On my visits to South Africa in the 1990s, I was horrified to realize that almost every black South African that I queried had been directly touched in some way by the long-reaching arm of the National Party's apartheid government. Everyone had a brother or an aunt or a neighbour that had been jailed, beaten or even killed. There were so many stories to tell, and all within a thirty-year span. In my mind, I can imagine that the people who grew up in the Gold Coast era of Ghana would have had similar stories to tell, and unfortunately spanning a much larger time frame. Generation after generation would have dealt with the presence of slave traders in their midst, or even worse, tribesmen who were cooperatives for the traders, earning some copper or gold in return for handing their own people over.

I had only been in West Africa for a couple of days when I started learning about the slave trade in ways that touched me far more than any university research project ever could have. The National Museum in Accra was hosting a special exhibit while I was there, something I wasn't aware of until I arrived. In retrospect, I'm incredibly thankful that I stayed the extra day in the city in order to visit. It was a lesson in humility for me.

The museum itself was on private, serene grounds, with rock-lined paths and an armless statue of Kwame Nkrumah, Ghana's father of independence. It was almost as if the exterior setting was designed to lull the visitor into feeling safe and comfortable, giving the exhibit on the inside all the more impact. As I stood in front of each glass case or display and read the descriptions, the full implication of what I was seeing hit me full force in the face. How could one race treat another so despicably? At that moment, I didn't even want to face up to it. I was looking at the history of my ancestors, and it was evil. I felt embarrassed, mortified even, to be white.

It was a very powerful experience, heightened by the fact that I was surrounded by a group of curious African children, their beautiful faces turned upward at me. With adoration, they followed me from room to room, waiting for me to read to them, and asking me questions about myself. Whatever they thought about the slave trade, and the cruelties that the white man had inflicted upon their tribes all those years ago, it didn't translate into any lack of trust or innocence in their demeanors. Oh, please, let it stay that way! I thought to myself.

The first town that I stopped in after leaving Accra was Cape Coast. Its fort was one of several that had been named a UNESCO World Heritage site.

After checking in at a hotel, I spent the early part of my day wandering through the rest of Cape Coast. I wanted to save my visit of the fort for last, a mental and emotional finale of sorts. When I eventually arrived at the front gates, it was about 3 o'clock. I was told that a tour would be starting within minutes, so I stood off to one side of the courtyard with several other tourists, among them, an African American woman and her daughter.

Considering the significance of this place to their origins, I thought that they seemed remarkably casual and collected. They were snacking on biscuits and a baggie o' juice that they'd bought at a market, the girl complaining about something or another. We could've been at a movie theatre, a Disney premiere for that matter, for the lack of unease that they were displaying. Did they understand where they were? They must have understood; they'd travelled thousands of freaking miles to get there! Maybe I was just being overly sensitive, allowing myself to get worked up over this place.

Our guide started off by telling about the courtyard, but then wasted no time in taking the group down to the first of four rooms in the basement. As I stood in the pitch-black, stiflingly-hot, acrid chamber of one of the slave dungeons, I felt utterly powerless. With a warning, the guide slammed the heavy, wooden door shut, leaving us in complete darkness. Every fraction of light had been eradicated, save for one tiny square high up on the wall. I imagined being held captive in the small rectangle of a room that had once been a holding pen for up to 1,500 men or women at one time, and I was physically sickened. Everyone was dead quiet, including the mother and daughter, their casual banter having evaporated at the start of our descent. There couldn't possibly have been anything else that could have demonstrated the horribleness of the slave trade like standing in that prison, its walls still bearing the scratches and etchings of its former inmates.

Back in the day, the prisoners' joy at being let out of the dungeon would have been short-lived. From there, they were led, shackled, through two massive and imposing wooden gates — the "Doors of No Return" — and onto ships bound for America or the Caribbean or wherever. The destination made no difference. It wasn't the start of something new for these unfortunate souls, it was the end of everything. Many of them never even survived the journey.

After our tour was over, I went upstairs to the open deck of the fort, where the cannons were still lined up, one after another, and I looked out over the ocean. My day was done. I wanted a drink. There was supposed to be a bar and restaurant next door to the castle, but it had burnt down only a month earlier, according to one of the locals. I made my way back to the hotel, taking the back streets because they were quieter, and I didn't feel much like looking anybody in the eye at that moment.

The slave trade, to me, is one of the most troubling of historical atrocities. It wasn't a war, where two sides plan, mobilize and engage in combat, it was a spiritual genocide. Human beings were ganged up on, captured, and taken away, tens of thousands of them. Nazi Germany, the Killing Fields of Cambodia, even the tribal wars that go on all over Africa today, they are about something different. At the center of those conflicts are elements of ethnicity or religion, and attempts at gaining power for one kind at another's expense. The slave trade was about neither of those things, though. It was about money. Using one group of people, perceived to be less intelligent, more vulnerable, to obtain cash rewards. Profit. And it was all perpetrated by those who thought themselves to be civilized.

In the 1600s, in the 1700s and the 1800s, the Africans that were taken as part of the slave trade never had a chance to defend themselves against their white foes. They likely never had a chance to say goodbye to their families, either. Standing inside the walls of one of the many massive slave forts in Ghana, I had the chance, plenty of time, in fact, to whisper a quiet apology before I departed.

# Chapter 5
# The Balance Between Primates and Progress

In addition to Tania, the doctoral candidate that was a long-term boarder at the Boabeng-Fiema Monkey Sanctuary, there was also a Peace Corps volunteer named Dan. He divided his time between four villages in the area, riding his bike sometimes 30 or 40 kilometres a day to go from one to the next. From what I remember, he'd been there for about a year, or half of his contract term, at the time of my visit.

One of the major projects that Dan was involved in was figuring out how to bring electricity to the Boabeng and Fiema villages. He acted largely as a facilitator, working with all of the local stakeholders, the national government departments, and several international agencies, some that had funded the sanctuary in the past and others that might eventually come on board to help fund the new infrastructure.

As with most things in Africa, this whole process was taking some time. There were several government ministries involved, and with the overlapping of jurisdictions, it made for many cooks in the kitchen. On the funding side, grant agencies, in general, have high expectations of their recipients when it comes to planning and reporting, and ask for a lot of supporting information before making any cash commitments. This may have been slowing things down even further. In this particular case, the proposal that was on the table was for the construction of underground power lines that would snake neatly along the side of the road, right through the monkey sanctuary.

Although the villagers liked this plan, they were getting impatient. They felt that it would be much quicker and cheaper to install above-ground power lines, and they wouldn't have to wait for donor money to proceed. Dan told me that a type of mass mentality had developed to support this idea in Boabeng and Fiema, but most of their arguments were founded in rumour and misinformation. Unfortunately, some of the villagers had already started to take matters into their own hands, and trees were being cut down in wide berths along the roadways to make room for the power lines.

Had it not been for the fact that they lived in the middle of a monkey sanctuary, this latter scheme would have also been fine. As it happened, though, the Mona and black and white Colobus monkeys that swung high amongst the treetops would be in great danger of connecting with the uninsulated conductors. It would mean an immediate death for them.

The work that Martha's father and countless other people had done almost thirty years prior to protect these little creatures would all be for naught if the villagers continued to proceed on this shortened timetable. To be fair, though, for them the thought of being able to easily run lights and music and cooking stoves was a pretty great temptation. To be able to live without everything being battery-dependent or candlelit, it would be pure heaven, I'm sure. Having enjoyed the sanctuary so much, though, I felt a certain measure of distress that summer, knowing that the long-term resolution was unclear at the time of my departure. I could only hope that their centuries-old religious reverence of the monkeys would prevail amongst the villagers, and that the international attention that the sanctuary was getting would bolster both their pride and their patience.

At this current juncture in time, I still don't know exactly how or when the Ministry of Energy would have connected the villages of Boabeng and Fiema to the national power grid. A recent article that was posted to an African news website, though, details delays to plans to deliver electricity to other villages in the same district because of the discovery of monkeys in those surrounding areas, too. There is even discussion of creating additional sanctuaries. Villagers have agreed to up to a two year delay in receiving power so that insulated conductors may be installed to replace the bare conductors that were originally put in place.

The recent release of this information bodes well for the hundreds of monkeys in Boabeng and Fiema, and my guess is that the end solution there met the needs of both people and primates. It also indicates an interesting shift of opinion in this region of Ghana. In developing countries around the world, rural inhabitants often face such a difficult struggle just to achieve day-to-day subsistence that they don't adopt long-term views in terms of preservation and sustainability. Here, not only are villagers putting their needs for electricity second to the protection of their local animals, but they are also sacrificing prized farmland at the same time. It seems that they are making a pretty reasonable attempt at balancing their community's progress with living alongside a creature that they at one time may have hunted.

# Chapter 6
# The Good, The Bad, and The Wicked

## 21 May 2001: Bouaké, Côte d'Ivoire

Hi all, how goes it? Well, it has been a while, non? But once outside of Ghana, e-mail service is practically non-existent in West Africa it seems. Plus there is this French keyboard issue, so please excuse the typos and punctuation problems. Y'all will be gettin a spate of e-mail from me when I am back in Accra cos boy do I have some stories to tell!! And thanks to all of you who have been sending me news and updates much appreciated!! Sorry about the layoffs, congrats on new family members, and yay, the NDP is finally gone!!

Anyway, I wanted to tell you a story now about a woman named Martha. People are always asking me what it is about Africa that I like so much, seeing as this is my 3rd trip to this continent (4th if you count Egypt, which I don't, really). I always give some semi-intangible answer, "You know, the people, the culture, the music..." Well, here is a better example.

I may have mentioned Martha before. We shared a car in Ghana from Nkranza to Boabeng village. As we went, she asked me where I was going, and I told her I was going to stay with the caretakers Alfred and Bea at the monkey sanctuary. "Ah," she said, "Bea is my cousin. They will take good care of you." I said that I was excited about going into the forest in the morning to see the monkeys. "Yes," she said, "it is a very special thing." The next day, after I had done my forest walk with the ranger, I went into the village and landed up on Martha's porch. We talked about this and that, kids, school, and life in Ghana. I raved about the sanctuary, which is a joint UNDP, Peace Corps, and EC project, so no small undertaking. She brought out a couple of photo albums for me which were done by a German photojournalist when he had been taking photos for periodicals.

The pictures were amazing, and I thought it interesting that he had made up these two albums for Martha, but anyway. We talked some more, I met her sisters and her son, and eventually her mother. I asked if her father also stayed there. "Yes," she said, "It is my father who created the sanctuary." My jaw dropped. I wasn't struck so much by the content of this information as I was by the fact that it had taken her a day and a half to tell me. You see, this is an African. They have a great deal of pride, but it is so beautifully tempered with quiet humility. There are no bragging rights, no grandiose displays of ego. Each day that has past is finished, and each day forward is a new one. Simple.

Not to say that ego is non existent, however. It must play some part each and every time that I am approached by an African man who presumptuously believes that I'd somehow want to play a part in helping him get a job in Canada, securing him a visa, or marrying him. I mean, these guys really seem to think that they have something to offer, too.

At first, I just politely laughed it off. After a while, getting more irritated, I started firing back with things like, "okay, so what exactly is in it for me?" and "why would I want to marry you?" And still it goes on. I feel a tirade building. A couple more weeks of this and the conversation is going to go something like this... "Bonjour. Yes, it is very hot today. My name? It's Laura. No, Laura. Laura. And you? Bambayame? But I can call you Mike. Okay. I'm from Canada. Yes, it is very nice there. Oh, you want to marry a Canadian woman? I see. No, I'm not married. You want to marry me? But why? We just met! Ah, because I'm so beautiful. No, Mike, beautiful is a woman who doesn't have to trim her nose hairs every two weeks. I'm not shittin you, it could really get to annoy a guy after a while. Oh, you think you'd make a good husband, hey? Because you'd stay around all the time? Ah, well, that's certainly a bonus. But you know, Mike, Western women have a slightly higher set of expectations than what you're used to, I think. Six cows, you say? Okay, Mike, but what about tech shares? You know, Cisco, Lucent etc? No? Well, you know, the girls won't even consider you unless you have a stock portfolio. Are you good in bed, Mike? Because you have to be able to perform there, too. I once broke up with a guy because he wasn't too great in the sack (okay, also because he had a tendency of closing his eyes when he spoke, thus closely resembling Mr. McGoo, and he reverted to baby talk when he thought he'd done something to annoy me, but whatever). Mike, do you know what cunnilingus is? Cunnilingus? C-U-N... No? Well. Then, you're definitely not marriage material for a Western woman. How about cooking. Do you like to cook, Mike? Because nowadays, it's a 50-50 job. And there'd be no maize or cassava in my house, Mike. What? Oh, okay, no problem. Ya, it was nice talking to you, too. Seeeeeeee ya!!!"

From Bouaké, Côte d'Ivoire,
Laura

P.S. Jules, do you want to send an edited version to Dad? I think you should cut out the word shit.

# Chapter 7
# Lead, and I Will Follow

Côte d'Ivoire is worthy of some story-telling, since I didn't get into much about it in my e-mails. I spent a total of about three weeks there. It is what I would call a "thought-provoking" country. It had more of a police and army presence than any of the other countries I visited, more visible corruption, more chronic political disturbances, more children in the streets instead of in school, more urban violence in the cities, more grit, and more of an edginess to it.

Evidence of the giddiness of the 1960s, when independence from European powers was fresh and each new African state was intent on making its statements through creative capital projects, was highly evident in Abidjan. Buildings were large, sometimes oddly-shaped and gilded or with mirrors, parks were fountained and manicured, streets were double-and triple-laned.

When the money dried up, the euphoria ended. Seeing Abidjan as it is now is like looking at an ageing movie star. No amount of makeup in the world will make it look as it once did; it needs the whole facelift. Now, as with Nairobi, Johannesburg and Lagos, a large number of rural and regional migrants have come to stay in Abidjan, and urban poverty has given rise to all sorts of other ills — crime, pollution, and the underground economy. There are several neighbourhoods that seem to have exceeded their optimal occupancy limits. Teeming with people, the streets and markets are like a sea of bodies, constantly moving. To be in the middle of it all is to be swept up in its flow, willingly or not. I stayed in one of these crazy, crowded and loud areas: Adjamé.

When I first disembarked from (or more accurately, spilled out of) the tro-tro that I had boarded on the Ghanaian side of the dotted line, there was immediately a crowd of men swarming around me, offering services, directions and God knows what else. I couldn't understand them, and I was embarrassed to tell them how incredibly rusty my French was, already thinking to myself that I was a complete fool for venturing into a Francophone zone when I hadn't uttered a word in that language for a dozen years. I had no idea where I was, or how I was going to find the hotel I'd selected from the guidebook. I wanted to just stand there for a moment and think, just breathe and formulate even one clear thought pattern in my brain, but their deluge of offers continued.

I often tell people that I have a guardian angel with me when I travel, some kind of spiritual force or being that keeps me from real harm and only ever lets me fall just so far into that hole of destitution before swooping in and scooping me to safety. She was with me that day. My feet started to move, and I went down the street looking left and looking right, every now and again feeling the brush of a moving vehicle against me as I manoeuvred my way towards I-don't-know-what. Maybe 300 metres along, I saw the sign for the hotel down one of the side streets. "Oh my God, it's right here?" I thought, once again surveying the layers of chaos that surrounded me and feeling some resultant trepidation. "But yay, it's right here!" I thought, filled with gratitude and delight over not having to move another inch.

Having secured a bed for the night, my thoughts turned to my next mission — exchanging money. It was late on a Friday after-noon, banks would be closed for two days, my Visa card never seemed to work in the ATMs, my U.S. cash was precious and lim-ited, and I'd only changed a small amount of cedis into CFAs at the border. Back in the madness of the streets, I was in the same flustered position as before, only now, time was of the essence. One of the same guys who had approached me earlier must have sensed a new-found opportunity, and he suddenly appeared by my side. This time I gratefully acknowledged his presence, and started rippling the pages of my phrase translation book. "Je veux…..aller…..a la banque… ." The sentence trailed off as I meekly waited for a sign of recognition of what I was requesting to appear on his face. I tried again. "J'ai….. besoin….l'argent….CFAs." I need money! This time he got it. He motioned for me to follow him. What choice did I have?

The likelihood of losing him in the crowded passages was slim, for he was like a young, black Frankenstein, tall and long-limbed, eyes dark and dull. I was silently hoping that the route would be a direct one, so that if he were to disappear as quickly as he'd appeared, I could at least find my way back. Alas, we took a series of turns and walked for close to half an hour, the man with all the time in the world, but no money, and the woman with neither.

The bank was closed, and it didn't have an ATM that I could try. My reaction was calm. I had expected that from the start of our walk, but had figured that it was my last hope. I remembered then that we had passed a travel agency not far back, on the main boulevard. This time I motioned for him to follow me.

The agency employees were somewhat surprised at my request, but after some backroom consultation, agreed to change some U.S. cash into CFAs for me. The rate wasn't good, about 14 percent less than what I would've got in a bank, but I almost wept with gratitude when they handed me the cash. Having money in my pocket was one of the things that made me feel, at that point, like I had some small measure of control over my life. That, and being able to sit in my suffocatingly hot and dingy hotel room and play The Tragically Hip on my portable CD player and speakers. It was something, at least.

The walk back to my hotel was somewhat less angst-ridden for me. It wasn't that I had developed any sort of trust in my companion, in fact I probably should have been even more leery than before as he had now seen my hidden treasure: the money belt around my waist. The day had worn me down, however, and as a result my guard had also come down somewhat. Either that angel must have still been riding along on my shoulder, or 'Frank' was even more docile than he appeared, for I didn't end up mugged and beaten in any back alleys and we arrived back at our starting point without incident.

Would I venture as far as saying that Frank was a good samaritan? Mmmmm, no, I don't think so. His kindess was definitely spurred on by the hope for compensation in return for his guidance. I didn't mind, though. He'd had the free time, and he'd done me a great favour. I tipped him with enough change to get a cold drink before he rejoined his comrades on the corner to pass the remainder of the day.

# Chapter 8
# Breasts: Not Such a Big Deal

## 27 May 2001: Bamako, Mali

I love that about Africa!! Women are whipping boobs out all over the place to feed their limitless babies, so they are really just so passe that nobody ever stares at mine. How refreshing is that?

Hi everybody! How goes it? A quick thank you to all of those who have been helping me with my errands and housekeeping at home — it is much much much appreciated.

I have been in Bamako, the capital city of Mali, for 3 nights now and will be here for another two. It's quite a cool city, actually, as the Lonely Planet puts it, "Bamako has buzz." Anyway, I arrived on Thursday night, and Friday was a national holiday, so I have to wait until Monday for the embassies to reopen so I can get my Burkina Faso visa. Thank God I made it to the bank on Thursday, with 30 minutes to spare, is all I can say!!

I have been enjoying Mali so far much more than Côte d'Ivoire. I mean, the places that I went in C.D. were beautiful, and I spent a couple of unforgettable nights in a traditional village after being invited by a fellow I met in Man, but all in all I found the people not very friendly, and I have retagged C.D. to stand for Corrupt and Dishonest. I have never been through more police roadblocks in my life!! Every 80 kilometres or so. Invariably after which we'd always lose one person off the minibus that didn't have the right papers and not enough money to pay the bribe either.

While Abidjan is called the Paris of West Africa and is the most developed city in the region (so I did find my contact lens solution there but let's laugh about this one — I paid $48 Cdn for 480 millilitres, what would have cost me 8 bucks at home. My fellow myopic friends, can you even imagine paying $48 for solution?) there are many, many traditional villages in the country.

All the food is pretty much made on site — peeling and pounding the cassava, getting the palm oil from the trees, growing the pimentos that add flavour. Actually the gifts that I took for the village elders, as instructed by my host, were bonbons and Maggi bouillabase broth cubes, which just make people's faces light up when you hand those suckers out. I was given a gift too, a bag of green stuff that I was told to sprinkle on my food to make me strong. I tried it once, and then hucked the bag, opting to not be carrying around unidentified leaves when I went through roadblocks and border crossings.

I watched the women in those villages work so hard I couldn't even believe it. What a life. And it all seems so preordained. What options or choices do they have? None. Do they even dream about escaping to something else, I wonder? Oh, it would drive me mad, living there. And yes, much, much, much female circumcision in those places. I was quite deflated when I realized just how difficult it would be to make inroads into changing traditions like that. Really, really difficult.

Back to the present, I will be heading out from Bamako and on to Djenne, home of the world's largest mud building in the form of a spectacular mosque, then Mopti, then trekking for 3 days in Dogon Country, where I will hire a local guide to take me from village to village, sleeping on the rooftops.

These villages in Dogon are fascinating, with most of the houses built into a rock escarpment. I can't wait. After that, Burkina Faso. In the meantime, I am enjoying being in the city, having e-mail, a restaurant (one) that cooks Western food, and all those other general things that you don't get once you leave an African capital. Although I must say, I happened upon a Dove ice cream bar in the shop of an Elf petrol station in Korhogo, C.D. (petrol stations are quite well-stocked in Africa). That was a happy find. Thank you France, for the imports.

So that's all for now!

From friendly Bamako,
Laura xoxo

# Chapter 9
# The Receiving Line

There was a chunk of time, several weeks in May, when I was not able to send any e-mail. This period stretched from when I left the city of Abidjan, in Côte d'Ivoire, to when I arrived in Bouaké, a city in the center of the country. The lack of Internet cafés was unfortunate, because it was an event-filled part of the trip.

Along that route, I touched down in the sleepy fishing village of Sassandra for four or five very enjoyable days and nights. After the sensory deluge of Abidjan, it was pure heaven, and I didn't even want to find a communication link to the outside (not that there was one, anyway). The only disturbance to my otherwise serene existence was that the so-called security guard at my water-side hotel had decided that it was completely acceptable to let a persistent young man named Bobsea past the front gate and into the complex every night. From there, my would-be suitor would assume his post outside my door, begging for me to open it so that he could give me a book or some hand-picked flowers. One night he kept insisting that he was going to stay with me that night. Generally, after a few minutes of telling him that he was barking up the wrong tree, I'd eventually fall asleep, and he'd go home. And so it would go.

Heading north-west from there, I spent about six nights in and around the town of Man. This day-long journey from Sassandra involved so many tro-tro shuffles that I wasn't even able to go to the bathroom for 16 hours. The van would stop at some roadside transport junction, someone would motion for me to get off, I'd trust in their judgment and go, some driver-to-driver negotiation would take place, and then someone else standing beside another van would call me over. "Yeah, we'll take the white girl." I felt like cattle. Mainly concerned with getting my backpack off of one roof rack and onto the next, I didn't even have time to scope out a toilet or well-concealed bush. Good thing I was dehydrated.

The hilly, western region of Côte d'Ivoire is noted not only for being the home of the political movement that led the coup d'état of 1999, but also for its traditional theatrical dance and story-telling culture. According to my guidebook, Man would be a good jump-off point for getting out to the small, nearby villages to witness some of these arts.

As would often happen, I didn't get into town until late at night; this time it was around 11:30 p.m. I knew which hotel I wanted to go to. I also knew that I'd be staying there that night whether it was good or bad, because my weary bones would have refused any further traipsing around to locate the best option. It turned out that this particular lodging, Hôtel Mont Dent, fell in the budget category that was especially attractive to prostitutes.

Once I had booked in, I passed by several 'non-traditionally dressed' women who were lounging around in the lobby area. The funny thing was that they all greeted me. That didn't often happen with African women. I was usually greeted by the men, but met with suspicious stares or looks of discomfort from the women, who weren't quite used to seeing other women out and about doing whatever the hell pleased them at any particular time of the day, like I was doing. Prostitutes, already having fallen outside the norms of their society, perhaps felt that they had more in common with me, who was also outside the norms of their society, than with their own native counterparts.

At any rate, it was always nice to stay in friendly surroundings so I appreciated their acceptance. The room turned out to be pretty reasonable as well, facing into a lovely garden courtyard. I ended up staying there for several nights, and was quite happy, barring the night where one of the girls got into a knock-'em-down drag-'em-out fight with a client at 2:30 in the morning. It went on for about twenty minutes, and at the end of it, I gave the victory to her. She had a mean upper cut, alright.

There was one little-used and dusty tourism office in the town of Man. If you went by and stood outside the locked front door long enough, somebody would call for someone else, who would run off to find somebody else, who would then eventually turn up and present themselves as the town's tourist guide. This is how I met Mikhael. He was 25 years old, had graduated from high school (which meant he could read and write, unlike most of his peers), and had enough money in his pocket to get a dinner of bread and egg and buy a cigarette or two from the street hawkers. I really don't know how he came up with cash for the next day's bread, egg and cigarettes.

Planning a day trip with Mikhael to some of the villages around the area took a great deal of paper-napkin negotiating over instant Nescafés in a corner café. The two show-stoppers to closing the deal were transportation (I'd need to hire a private car to go where I wanted to go), and payment for the stilt-dancing show (about 20 musicians and dancers would have to be assembled for a performance). Since there were no other tourists around to share the cost with, the whole burden was going to fall on me, but it also meant that they would be performing just for me. Knowing that I might never be back to wander those roads again, and that my USD $60 could go a long way towards feeding a multitude of families within the village, I agreed to Mikhael's terms.

We met the next morning near the tourism office, whereupon he led me around the corner to a waiting car and our driver, a quiet fellow named Bamba. I'd already stopped at a shop and purchased my gifts of bouillon cubes and hard candies for the chiefs, elders and children, respectively, so we were all set to go, or so I thought. About 20 kilometres out of town, I realized that I'd forgotten to bring my passport. With Côte d'Ivoire being notorious for its frequent roadblocks and intimidating document checks, we decided that it would definitely not be prudent to carry on without it. Bamba wheeled the car around and we went back to the hotel so I could retrieve my passport before setting off again.

While we had to get to the dancers' village early in the morning to give ample notice of our request for the performance, the stilt dancing itself had to wait until the end of the day, when all the men returned from working in the coffee fields. That left us with about seven hours of unstructured, unplanned time, which I would soon find out would be passed in a very day-in-Africa kind of way.

While Mikhael went from hut to hut negotiating the details of the evening performance with some of the men, I hung back near the car with Bamba and took in the scenery, not sure if it was the appropriate time for me to come forward and present myself. The region was incredibly beautiful. Just to look at the dense, dark greenness of it made me want to run into the hills and spend the day weaving criss-cross patterns through the ropey vines and fanned-out trees.

It was about 40 degrees Celsius, though (that's 110 in Fahrenheit). I couldn't even find comfort sitting dead still in the shade. Where were the creeks and rivers when you needed them? I think I would have immersed myself in the water clothing and all, had it been available. And had I been traveling deluxe instead of economy, I would have carried bottled water both for drinking and for pouring over my head. At nearly USD $1 a bottle in some places, though, it was reserved strictly for consumption, as I needed a minimum of three a day.

Touring the village itself could wait until later in the day when it cooled down some, so we set off in the car again. About a half hour down the road was the mid-size town of Touba. Mikhael must have figured that I'd be getting hungry soon, because he instructed Bamba to drop us at an outdoor lunch counter-style restaurant. Bamba did so, and then disappeared with the car. Apparently we weren't going anywhere else in a hurry.

Once I'd made the difficult choice between eggs or African-Italian spaghetti, their only offerings, I realized that I'd attracted the interest of all the other lunch counter patrons. They were keen to talk, and I really wanted to oblige. It was like talking to the Muppets, though! There was the Swedish chef character, sing-songing his way through his sentences, words running one into another. There was Animal, rumbly, aggressive and nonsensical. And there was Beaker, high-pitched and, well, yeah, high-pitched. Behind the counter was a kinder, gentler Frank character (one of the old men from the balcony in the Muppet Show). He filled in the gaps when the others stopped speaking, providing small talk, one-liners, and smiles. Together, they were an ensemble that all understood each other perfectly, but had me turning my head from one to the other in confusion, trying to answer their questions when required and hoping that I laughed at the appropriate times.

When I tired of this, I politely excused myself and made my way to the back of the building, looking for Mikhael. I understood then why he had chosen that particular spot as our drop-off point. There were two or three large, leafy trees, and several benches and chairs spread out beneath them. Mikhael occupied one of them, eyes closed, dozing in the afternoon heat. Using my daypack as a pillow, I stretched out on one of the benches and decided to do the same.

Bamba eventually reappeared. He stopped to discuss this-and-that (spoken in Africa exactly like I've spelled it, as one long word) with some of his acquaintances before we all piled back in the car. Once at the village, we passed the remaining time by walking around very slowly, weaving a path between the round, thatched-roof huts and visiting with the women as they pounded cassava, brushed freshly-picked cotton so it was ready for spinning, or carried water from the wells. Each activity was a common daily task in the village, and I watched in fascination at the amount of physical energy that was expended to achieve something that would just have to be repeated all over again the next day.

The image of the young girls working to refine their local grains from a raw state into flour is one that has remained particularly vivid in my mind. Three of them would stand around one receptacle, a wood basin that looked a little bit like a djembe drum with the skin removed from the top. Each held a long stick. They took turns hammering the grain, going around their little circle, 1-2-3, in perfect, unbroken rhythm. When they raised their sticks up in the air, their backs arched like bows and they looked like beautiful statues, but then just as quickly, they brought their arms down with a force that I would have never expected from those so diminutive. Bang, bang, bang. It was a noise that in the next few days I would both wake and fall asleep to.

As dusk approached, the sound of the drums alerted us to the start of the performance, so we made our way in the direction of their sound. I was led to the center of the village by the two or three children that were hanging on to each of my arms. They had been attached in this way since we'd first arrived. Funny, because I think if this had ever happened to me at home, I would have shaken them off like pesty flies. Here, it seemed so very charming, and I felt somewhat honoured to have this entourage. When I would stop with Mikhael to observe or talk with someone, the kids would trace patterns up and down the backs of my hands with their fingers, following the lines of my prominently blue and bulging veins. They could not see the flow of blood so vividly in their own skin. It must have seemed quite odd.

When we arrived in the square, the first dance had already begun. A dozen or so women dressed in white shirts or sarong wraps and dark skirts, some with white paint on their faces, were moving slowly but rhythmically in a circle. Six or seven men were lined up along the back, beating on the hourglass-shaped djembe and elliptical kponlogo drums. I didn't know what it all meant, but it seemed like an introductory number of sorts, kind of like the background music that plays before the lights go down at a theatre show. It went on for at least ten minutes; long enough for many of the villagers, more than a hundred, I'd say, to arrive and find a perch from which to watch.

Immediately noticing a row of benches towards the rear of the area, I started towards them. Mikhael redirected me, however. It turned out that proper etiquette required that I pass through a receiving line of the village elders before taking my seat at the back of the square. I began at the far end, and one by one, each rose to shake my hand and exchange a greeting of sorts in their local tribal language. I was unusually unsure of myself as I made my way through, and kept my head bowed in deference, both out of respect and the exercise of caution.

There were times in West Africa when I performed the social act or action that seemed expected of me, even though I wasn't entirely sure of its intent or implication. On this occasion, however, it was crystal clear to me that the elders were not there to greet and welcome me to the performance. Their body language was different than what I had seen before when being introduced to someone. They were very serious, and stood upright and still. I was most definitely the one making the offering, as if to say thank-you for allowing me into their village. These were the people who held the power in this community, I realized afterwards, and not just in a figurehead or ceremonial type of way. They had real power.

Having bowed to the last of the elders, I settled into a spot on one of the benches. Five or six men, dressed completely ordinarily, came out for the second dance, which Mikhael described to me as 'acrobatics.' I had seen greater agility among the hackeysack players on Kitsilano Beach in Vancouver, so I wasn't overly impressed. They just didn't seem to be trying very hard! When I saw the central figure of the third dance, however, I knew that the efforts to coordinate this evening had all been worthwhile.

Quietly looming just to the side of me, waiting for his queue, was the stilt dancer. He was freakishly tall, of course, and was shrouded in a black cape and full head mask that made his features completely indistinguishable. By this time, night had fallen, so the only light was from a fire at the back of the square. This only added to his mystique as he crossed back and forth in sweeping steps. Accompanying him were four support men, literally there to catch him if he fell while attempting any of his numerous spins and jumps. My earlier nervousness had dissipated, and I jumped up and circled the stage area, shooting pictures from different angles and moving in as close as I could to capture an image of this amazing and strange spectacle.

Once the stilt dancer had exited from the square, Mikhael shook me out of my safe role as an observer of the performance by motioning for me to get up and take center stage. "Go," he said, "Go and dance!" Not wanting to cause a scene (or be disrespectful to my hosts) I gave him the death glare before taking a few tentative steps out into the middle.

One of the acrobats handed me a horse-hair 'duster' (that's the best way I can describe it) and then moved to the side, as if he was doing me a favour by giving me the whole area to myself. What the hell, I thought, you'll never see any of these people again! And so I danced. The village watched, and I danced. I waved the duster around, swoosh swoosh, back and forth in the air. You are smooth, Laura. You are cool and fluid and not foolish-looking at all. I thought of the women that I'd once laughed at in a nightclub as they danced in circles around the pile of handbags on the floor, looking like they'd forgotten every style and move that came after Flashdance. Suddenly, I felt kindred.

After what seemed like an eternity (but was probably only a minute), one of the acrobat guys joined me on stage. From then on I just mimicked his moves until the drumming made an imperceptible change to a different rhythm, at which time I figured I could safely use the 'end of song' excuse and get the heck out of there. There were a few small hoots and claps from the audience, more in support than in laughter, I think. They weren't rolling in the aisles, at least.

Later that night, spending one of many evenings in my hotel room, it struck me what the dynamic between the village elders and the younger residents meant to change and development in African society. When making decisions or forming opinions on something, first and foremost, people listen to the chiefs and elders in their communities. As narrow a funnel of information and knowledge as it is, that is where they turn for direction and leadership. To do otherwise would be considered utterly disrespectful. While this continued homage is important in preserving the traditions and culture that add value to African society, it does not help with advancement in areas where old practices and beliefs have, realistically, hindered the health and education of Africa's people.

Further compounding the effects of this dynamic is the fact that the regular mediums of information that we in the Western world are used to — television, the Internet, a liberal school curriculum — are not widely available in Africa. Female circumcision, polygamy, literacy, and the plethora of other such issues that plague international development advocates around the globe are not discussed in village gatherings. Such topics are the focus of round table discussions at African universities and United Nations agencies.

Even though both African and Western educated minds are often aligned in their views of what should happen, what needs to happen, it is incredibly difficult to carry this information forward to the local village setting, and even more importantly, build the type of relationship required for people to trust the source. When information trickles in from other outside sources, people will still likely defer to the opinions of their elders, whom already have the trust and respect of the community. Even the city dwellers, who number in the millions, have adopted certain elements of Western culture, and are exposed to a wide variety of information, will still consult their elders upon returning to their rural homes for a visit. And so, year after year, things remain as they are, which is largely as they have been.

In many regards, African culture is deserving of our envy. There are so many beautiful things that are present in day-to-day life, old customs that they have held onto and sustained, that are nurturing of spirit and soul. Unfortunately, there are also some practices which are to the detriment of its people, the undervaluing of education and the mutilation of female genitalia amongst them, and these things warrant reevaluation. To conduct such a reassessment, and then perhaps to work at reshaping core beliefs and policies as a result, should not be ruled out as impossible. It would surely take an enormous amount of time, though, as there are so many towns and villages.

Africa has only been in its post-colonial 'free' period for 40-odd years, finally developing its own social policy and working in partnership with international development agencies and other agents of change. All in all, it is a process that is still in its early stages, with its own unique variables and circumstances. We may not live to see the end results of any significant shift, in fact, it's almost a given. If we put this into some historical perspective, however, and look at the span of eras, revolutions and evolutions across the length of a date-sensitive continuum, it's really not anything out of the ordinary.

# Chapter 10
# Showing My Best Side

After I had spent a paid day with Mikhael in the villages north of Man, he invited me to come to his home village of Santa for a few days as his guest. "It's not very far," he said, "but I only go home once a year to see my family." I thought this to be a strange admission, especially knowing that he had an abundance of spare time on his hands. After spending an entire day on the road trying to get there, though, I understood why.

We had to go about 115 kilometres north, only to backtrack about 65 of them again in the other direction. We moved at an absolute snail's pace, making stops that were sometimes just 50 metres apart to pick up or drop off people, cargo or livestock. Four or five hours were spent hanging around at a restaurant counter in the small town of Touba, waiting for the ramshackle vehicle that was the bus to fill up so it could depart for Ouanini.

Accompanying us was Mikhael's friend Manoi, who also came from the same village. Each took turns endeavouring to distract and entertain me, showing me the alligators that someone had caught and penned up at the back of their property, knocking mangoes from a tree and offering them as small gifts of consolation for the interminable wait. When we finally arrived at the village, the sun was disappearing behind the mountains. It had taken us nine hours to get to a place that was, as the crow flies, 45 kilometres from Man.

Whether it was necessary for Mikhael to do an immediate round of village greetings, or attend to some other aspect of the prodigal son's return home I'm not completely sure. He left me with the womenfolk of the family so that they could sort me out for a shower and disappeared off into the night with Manoi.

I was given a bucket of water and a bar of soap, and shown into a long, rectangular building (quite different from the traditional round thatch-roofed huts that covered most of the landscape in that region). The shower area — I won't call it a room, because it wasn't — was at the end of the dark hall, just an open space with one partially enclosed wall that offered about 16 inches worth of privacy. I stripped down, placing my belongings in the hall, and with my flashlight awkwardly inserted into its headband adapter, attempted to bathe. Of course, (of course), within minutes, the door to the house opened and a man entered, his flashlight beam projecting down the corridor and landing directly on my naked bits. My head whipped around in his direction — all I could do was hope that the cast of my headlamp temporarily limited his vision. He silently went off into one of the rooms, and I quickly dressed and fled, rejoining the circle of women outside.

I wondered afterward if that incident was ever repeated around the village. Was the man embarrassed? Did he keep it to himself, feeling ashamed or disrespectful for the ill-timed entry? Did he care at all? Or did the encounter become living legend amongst the village men — "Remember that day? The day when so-and-so saw the white woman's ass? It was pretty small! She must be from a poor family."

Truth be told, my rear end was quite a bit fleshier than many of the women around. The energy expended by me during years of desk jobs wouldn't even come close to the calories burned in a year of the hard labour that was their work output. And I doubt very much that anybody there thought my origins to be as humble as theirs. The nature of the climate kept me to a basic wardrobe of T-shirts, shorts, and sandals, so while my appearance was 180 degrees from the wool suit and leather briefcase that was my normal Monday-to-Friday attire for the latter half of the 1990s, as soon as they saw me pull out my camera or pick a CD for my Walkman, they knew that I was holding what was several years' worth of their income in my hands. Nobody treated me any differently for this, though, at least in the village of Santa.

That night, Mikhael, Manoi and I concentrated our round of visits on the most immediate family. I say this because, as it turned out, most of the village was family of some sort. Generations earlier, Santa, as with many settlements in the area, had been started by one man and his four wives (while polygamy was becoming less of the norm, it was still often practiced). Everyone that I met was incredibly gracious, clasping my hands through long, drawn-out greetings and welcoming me over and over again. I was unable to follow much of the conversation, as it was in local dialect, but every now and again they would make an effort to include me by speaking French, or Mikhael would lean over and give me a quick translation.

Aside from abandoning me when we first arrived, Mikhael was ever the gentleman. This was a very good thing, because as it turned out, the sleeping arrangements had him and I sharing a mattress when we eventually turned in after our visiting. He was ever the gentleman in that respect, too, except for an occasional wildly-flailing arm in my face when he swatted mosquitoes in his sleep.

When day came, we made many more stops, going up and down the rows, from hut to hut. All were sparsely decorated except for one somewhat common feature, posters of a military leader. "Who is that?" I asked Mikhael. He told me it was the man who led the big coup d'état in 1999. He was from that village, but, having been ousted himself, was now in hiding somewhere else in the area.

The particular poster that I was looking at when I asked about this man, General Robert Guei, was a collage of more than a dozen photos of him posing with various people, doing the look-important-for-the-camera thing. "He sure likes himself," I said to the woman of the house. "Ici, c'est moi! Et ici, c'est moi encore, et ici, regardez! Aussi, c'est moi!" Everybody laughed. It was a normal thing, though, for them to have politicians or military generals who led by developing a cult of personality. They either didn't recognize it, or just didn't question it all that much, and, living in the same village as an active rebel leader, they sure as heck didn't refuse when someone from his ranks offered them posters to adorn their walls.

Even after staying in Santa for three days and asking Mikhael repeated questions, I still couldn't be exactly sure who his father and mother were, or if I had met them at all. There were two elderly men (they were probably only 50, but looked 80) that we visited several times each day, and from what I could make out, it was a fairly obligatory thing. We would take our places sitting in a hammock or on some cushions, the elder would speak, and Mikhael would listen attentively. Occasionally, he would nod, or utter a few words in response. Most of the time, he just listened.

I never asked what the conversations were about, I just assumed that it was the Ivoirian village version of the parent-child talk — "It's time to start saving for your retirement," or "Have you changed the oil on your car lately?" — except in village context, with a spiritual undertone. The discussions were always serious, hence consistent with daily life in Santa. I do believe that Mikhael's family was happy to see him on this return home for a visit, but they showed it with great reservation. No hugs and kisses or exclamations of joy, just some small Mona Lisa smiles and pats on the shoulder. It's possible that their views of him changed when he originally left the village to go and live in the city (first in Abidjan, where he worked in a factory, then in Man, where he was essentially unemployed). Perhaps his parents didn't approve of his choices.

I remember one story that Mikhael told me, about how, when he was nine, he had to beg his father to allow him to continue going to school. He cried, he said. His father would have rather had him working around the village or selling bread and water in a nearby lorry park (the depots for buses and trucks in the bigger towns). In the end, he was allowed to continue through to graduation. As a young man, I believe that Mikhael had greater aspirations for his life than his father had had for his own, which would also explain why he hadn't married or had children yet, even though at 25 he was practically nearing middle age in African terms. It seemed fairly obvious to me, though, that after having spent several years in the cities, Mikhael was no longer the same as the 300 or so people that inhabited Santa, especially when sporting his cut-off jeans, a Labatt's Blue baseball cap that I had given him, and hand-me-down designer shoes from a French engineer who worked in Man.

Beyond doing the twice-a-day social hut crawl, our time was pretty much our own in the village. The heat kept me down during the greater part of the day, but on our second afternoon there, I went for a hike into the hills with Manoi. The landscape was lush and beautiful. Every now and then we'd pass somebody who was already coming back from a full day in the fields somewhere nearby, and I'd feel a twinge of guilt for being Western and slovenly by comparison.

On the third day, we were due to leave. As fantastic and unique as the experience had been, I was looking forward to being back in a hotel room that night, as I hadn't really had a moment alone since we'd been there. We had packed up our belongings and were preparing to say goodbye to some of the family members when Mikhael approached me. "Please, I need some money to give to my family," he said. Explaining that it was customary for a visiting family member to leave money with the male elders, he wanted me to spot him a couple of thousand CFAs as he hadn't any money of his own left. I handed it over without hesitation, as I had planned to give him 5 000 CFA anyway at the end of our journey as a gift for taking me as his guest.

The truck that carried us back to Ouanini was a decrepit, stinky diesel-burning contraption. It was obviously used for hauling cargo, but had also become passenger transport by default because there was little else on wheels in those parts. Being the only white female tourist to board the vehicle, I was spared the dust and heat of riding in the back and kindly given the only seat in the cab. We arrived at the town a couple of hours later. It was time to pay the driver. Manoi and I handed over our cash, but Mikhael just sheepishly stood there. It was then that he confessed to not having any money for his transport back to Man. That little bugger, I thought, spitting mad. Although he had invited me as his guest, Mikhael had known from the beginning that he could only afford to pay his own fare in one direction, and therefore was counting on me to front the cost of the return ticket.

I really didn't like that he had made that little detail a part of his plan. It made me feel like I was being taken advantage of, even though there was no question that I had the cash and could take care of the fares. I told him this on the next leg of our journey, scolding him for his deception. At first, Mikhael denied my charge, saying that fares had gone up, and he hadn't brought enough money with him to allow for the increase. Eventually, realizing that he'd been busted, he began to sulk and we didn't speak for most of the way from Touba to Man.

It wasn't until we'd reached our destination and Mikhael walked me back to my hotel that he offered up an apology and asked me to forgive him. I did, although not without some grousing and grumbling first. I knew that he was a good guy at heart, though. Perhaps he couldn't bring himself to bury his pride and just ask me up front if he could have some money. Putting my Miss Manners-conditioned feelings aside, I realized that the end result had still been a good one. I was lucky enough to experience a day (or three) in the life in an African village, and, for the first time in a long time, a young man was able to see his family.

# Chapter 11
# Random Thoughts

28 May 2001: Bamako, Mali

1. Silver jewellry looks pretty when you're tanned.

2. You've been in Africa too long when you wake up in the morning, see the giant cockroach that's spinning around on his back (probably because he fell off your bed), and instead of flinching, greet him with a "Hey, little buddy!"

3. Sure, you can wash your Teva sandals, but they never really lose their smell.

4. Blowing boogers out the side of your nose and onto the ground is inappropriate, I think.

5. When the taxi driver misunderstands your directions because your French is shite, it's not really your fault, he just wasn't listening.

6. It makes one wonder why, in a Muslim country, would there be a demand for pigs' feet?

Actually my French isn't that shite, I seem to actually remember quite a lot from those high school years. I can hold a conversation, anyway, doing phenomenally better if I'm the one that started it because then I know the context. I'm even thinking in French in my head, which is really terribly annoying because as it is I'm sadly lacking in English conversation yet even my subconscious seems determined to deprive me (there aren't many travelers at all this side of the world). Then I start berating myself, "stop it, think in English!" which is equally troubling because what do you do when you're traveling alone but not getting along with oneself?

It appears that I'm stuck in Bamako for a few more days, as the only guy in the Burkina embassy that can issue visas is traveling until Wednesday. Oh well, at least I like the city. I found another awesome restaurant in embassy row today (cuz it's the expat neighbourhood) that had a salad bar better than some of ours at home so way cool that was. I also bought an inordinate amount of silver in the artisan market today, though, so I shall be living on rice and sauce for a few days to compensate. Rice and sauce, rice and sauce, 20 cents!

I have so much enjoyed the opportunity to read while I am here. My love affair with words that I had when I was eight and read 24 books a month has started anew!! I am determined that when I return home in July, I am canceling my cable (having tried twice before, and getting talked out of it by those wily Rogers-Shaw people so that I ended up just going from the Combo package to Basic...). The latter half of 2001 is going to be called Educating Laura. I'm going to renew my subscription to the Economist, rent a whole bunch of classic movies, and leave the prime time garbage in my wake. (Chrissy, could you just tape The West Wing for me though?). And I'm going to Ikea to buy a bigger bookshelf. Yeah.

Well I guess I'll call it a night. Hope you're not getting tired of hearing from me! It's just so nice to have convenient (2 minutes from my hotel) and cheap e-mail. Mali is running on wireless. So much better than the dial-up in C.D.

Ciao for now, gang!
Laura

# Chapter 12
# 10 Things I Miss About Home

**29 May 2001: Bamako, Mali**

I'm in a lists mood.

This list does not include human beings or pugs. It is not in any particular order. It consists of but is not limited to the following:

1. The independence of cruising in my RAV-mobile, especially with my dear nephews in the passenger seats so I can ride in the HOV lane (and apparently Aunty says this every time, too).

2. Not having multi-legged creatures scuttle across my extremities, e.g. mice, cockroaches, lizards (all of which have, thus far).

3. Working Monday to Friday, 9 to 5. NOT!!

4. Dairy Queen Oreo Blizzards.

5. Spritzing on Issey Miyake or Carolina Herrera as my evening fragrance instead of DEET.

6. Sitting on chairs and toilet seats that aren't cracked and pinch my butt when I try to stand up.

7. Grocery shopping and cooking for myself. Did I just say that?

8. My Avon Pore Minimizing Mask.

9. Mushrooms. Mushroom omelettes, mushroom soup, mushroom burgers, grilled mushrooms to put over my BBQ'd steak, mushrooms in my pasta sauce. Oooohhhh, pasta. Linguini Vongole, Rotini Frutti di Mare, fettucine with pesto....

10. Not sharing most gastronomic undertakings with a half dozen or so flies.

Okay, 11 things. I really miss my washing machine. Wash, rinse, spin, voila!

It rained today in Bamako!! Yay! Okay, it was only for about a half hour or so, but it was better than nothing. Maybe I'll be able to sleep tonight without being drenched in a pool of sweat. It's amazing how little air-con there is in a town like this. I actually LIKE it that the banks take so long because it means that I get to stay in the air con for more time.

I'm quite chuffed with myself today because I picked up a copy of last week's Economist for $1.50 U.S. from a street hawker and the same issue was selling for over $5 in the book store at one of the big hotels (where I go to read all the latest Time, Newsweek etc. without actually buying them!!).

Turns out Colin Powell was here last week. Don't know what he was doing, but he was here. I went to the Canadian embassy yesterday looking for Globe and Mail newspapers and they didn't have anything in English at all. Not even an English speaking employee in the building!! So much for home front camaraderie. I'm starting to see a few more tourists around Bamako, but still not many. I've been hanging out with a Japanese woman that was staying where I am but there aren't many people there because its only a 2 room hotel of sorts and not listed in any guide books and I only found it through some guy on the street that walked me there. But man, there were NO tourists in C.D. Apparently tourism really dropped off after the coup d'état!

Speaking of war, things are really brewing strongly out here in a tri-country war of sorts between Sierra Leone, Guinea and Liberia. Its funny how the media publicizes certain conflicts and not others. We heard so much about Sierra Leone last year but nothing about Liberia at all, and it has been brewing for a decade there as well. It reminds me of Noam Chomsky's comparison of film footage taken of Cambodia and East Timor in the 70s, as in lots and none. But anyway, the war is spreading in the region, and it is written in the Economist that Mali, Côte d'Ivoire, Ghana, and Nigeria could all quite easily end up being involved. God the whole region could be in total destabilization. And thus far, the UN doesn't want to step in. They'll wait til the shit hits the fan, first. Anyway, the refugee impact is already quite visible — there are a lot of displaced persons, and families that have been separated. Very, very sad.

Anyway, my hour for today is up! I've become a regular e-mail junkie! Oh well, I won't have any again until I hit Ouagadougou in a couple of weeks time. I've bought a bus ticket to leave Bamako tomorrow for Mopti on a night bus, after I pick up my visa.

Talk to y'all tomorrow!
Laura

# Chapter 13
# We Drew the Borders

It appears that after laying low for almost two years, his military regime having been ousted in October 2000, Robert Guei yet again emerged with guns blazing in Côte d'Ivoire. Making another attempt to change the political landscape of the country, he led rebel troops in the takeover of Bouaké in September 2002, but was himself killed in one of the first days of fighting.

Although the coup attempt failed, the rebels held control of several towns in the northern half of the country for many months, and were later joined by two Liberian rebel groups who captured strongholds in the west. A new unity government has been put into place, the result of peace talks that were brokered by France, however sporadic violence continues throughout the country, even now. At this juncture, a good adjective for the political climate in the Ivory Coast would be 'fragile.'

This current round of fighting began for much the same reason as the overthrow in 1999. Several groups in the country complain that the government is still overly attentive to the small

Christian population (and to the Baoulé ethnic group) that reside largely in the southern half of the country, from Yamoussoukro and below. Inhabitants of the northern and western parts of Côte d'Ivoire, largely from the Mande group (and either Muslim or traditionalists), claim that they are treated as second-class citizens and receive fewer government transfer payments and subsidies than their southern counterparts.

Adding to ethnic tensions is the fact that a large number of the labourers that staff the coffee and cocoa farms of the western region come from other countries; Burkina Faso, Mali and Guinea. These immigrants are also feeling the resentment of local villagers and the rebel group, and attempts were made by their home countries to repatriate them when the level of violence escalated in 2002.

Civil wars and coups d'état are common in Africa, probably more so than anywhere else in the world, largely because this continent was almost completely partitioned and colonized by European imperialists. The people who drew the lines to create the borders gave little consideration to tribal regions and compatibilities, and the application of Western-style models of government has been stymied by the natural inclination of rulers to cater to the needs of the ethnic groups from which they come.

Often times, the largest ethnic group in a country will control much of the government, but may still only represent a small percentage of the total population, just because there are so many different ethnicities. Such is the case in Mali, where the Bambara make up only 23 percent of the country's inhabitants, but hold the lion's share of economic control and government offices.

While parts of East Africa can be considered somewhat homogeneous — they speak Swahili in large parts of Uganda, Kenya and Tanzania — in West Africa, there are hundreds of tribes, each with their own language, facial markings, and pride of origin. Some of these tribes literally straddle the borders that were drawn by the colonialists, their groups split in half by that imaginary line. It's hard to imagine, especially coming from a country like Canada, where we are all new transplants, mixed up amongst each other, only having arrived within the last two hundred years.

Causing even greater problems in Africa is the fact that the institutions that we so often take for granted here in the West — a sound judicial system, and separate and distinct police and military bodies, for example — were not given any time to develop prior to the transition from colony to independent state. Even now, these institutions are shaky at best. All in all, the results of having gone from being colonial daughter to new debutante have been less than optimal.

Ongoing conflicts on this continent have displaced hundreds of thousands of people, impaired attempts at development and now, more recently, all but destroyed tourism in some African countries. The people living there are helpless victims, even within their own homelands. It is not the majority — it is not even a substantial minority — that fuel these conflicts to the levels of violence that they eventually reach. As in any country, there is usually only a handful of power-hungry people with brash, unpopular ideas. In Africa, however, where one can be hard-pressed to find examples of good, moral leadership, they are quite easily able to turn these unpopular ideas into popular fronts by targeting an impressionable group of citizens — the youth.

Education systems have been largely ineffective in changing the tides of disenfranchisement. First off, not every one that wants to go to school can. There are high dropout rates, even at primary levels, because of fees for uniforms and books. Schools are also underresourced due to lack of public funding. Their materials are lacking, the teachers are poorly educated themselves, and the sheer number of people under the age of 18 far outstrips the availability of classrooms. Combine all of this with cyclical conditions of poverty and unemployment, and you have created an environment where young men and women are just plain frustrated.

At an age that can be characterized as hopeful in many other parts of the world, in Africa, you will find youth who are cynical about their future, and either keen or easily-swayed to join groups and pledge allegiance to causes that make them feel a part of something that might be a catalyst for change. Even their methods for effecting change are different than what you might find elsewhere. Lobbying, letter-writing and peaceful marching have little impact on the imbalances in the institutions that govern, so instead, they opt for something that will show more immediate results: military action.

Starting from about age 14, kids will don armbands and pick up guns with the same enthusiasm that those in other cultures display when joining baseball teams, social groups or university clubs; it makes them a part of something. They are provided with a feeling of camaraderie and a sense of purpose. And once their cause is achieved, whether by coup d'état or men in blue pin-striped suits holding formal round-table talks (witness South Africa), this group of young people doesn't necessarily come away well-adjusted and with a sense of accomplishment. Sometimes they are even worse off, marginalized once again, but under a different set of circumstances. And so they might pledge allegiance to a different group, perhaps a gang or a regional warlord or some other socially-subversive element that acts to divide people and resources rather than build communities.

I am always incredibly saddened and perplexed when I hear of, or witness, the resurgence of conflict in these areas. They are incredibly complex situations — many different ethnic groups, disproportionate representation at government levels, and corrupt leaders are often part of the dynamic, along with many other variables. Too often, I hear quick and perhaps unfair judgments of these situations from others, and I wish that more people would apply benefit-of-the-doubt in the short term and make a greater effort to learn about the dynamics in the long term. With all the information that we have access to, with airplanes going to all the places that they go, and the Internet showing us all the things that can be shown (and then some!), we still have far too vast a populace that uses simple and unrealistic criteria to decide what constitutes civilized or uncivilized society, and who is a beacon of democracy or bastion of terrorism.

At a community level, and sometimes even nationally, we try to counteract this momentum by building anti-racism campaigns and holding cultural festivals. How much does it help? People still hold fast to what they think they know, and only seek out new information and experiences if it doesn't make them too uncomfortable. We aren't always exactly the bravest of little warriors! Going beyond the comfort zone can be so exquisitely fun, though. Learning about different people, places and things around us isn't just enriching, it's practically necessary in this day and age. The term 'global village' didn't come about for nothing.

I'm a big fan of perspective when it comes to stuff like this. If we think that religion or culture or geographic location makes one society love their children or want peace any more or less than another then we are getting the wrong impression from our news sources. Yes, it takes a concerted effort to seek out better information and gain greater understanding of communities beyond our own, but it can be done. We can get on a plane and go find out for ourselves (yes, some people do this), take a history class, or read a few well-selected books (preferably presenting opposing views). And why should we bother? Because this is our world. This is our globe. East is going to overlap with West, and North will overlap with South. Physically, we have never really been isolated. Mentally, we create our own borders.

Sadly, not many places, least of all Africa, have had the benefit of centuries of peace in their homelands as we have had in Canada. In Côte d'Ivoire, there will be many other Robert Guei's who will mobilize the disenchanted and try to use extreme force to accomplish their goals. It will make it difficult to rebuild; one step forward might still end up in two steps back again. Somewhere, in the midst of all of the chaos, strife and bloodshed, I hope that they will eventually find a solution. When they do, it will be uniquely their own.

# Chapter 14
# 10 Things I Love About Africa

---

**30 May 2001: Bamako, Mali**

1. Mangoes — cheap and plentiful.

2. The precocious children who travel in packs of five or six, greet me with a Bon Soir, and shake my hand as they pass by. (These same precocious children usually end up annoying me when, after giggling and whispering for a couple of minutes, they come back to ask me for money. Please refer to 10 Things I Hate About Africa, to be published at a later date).

3. The red, red earth.

4. When I walk into a shop for the second or third time and they already know who I am and what I want before I even have a chance to ask for it.

5. The way that music can bring about an eruption of singing and dancing, anytime, anywhere — children on a

---

balcony, women by the side of the road, a man standing on the roof of a minibus.

6. That it gives inspiration to me. We should all find such a place.

7. Peugots, Peugots everywhere. (Non, Papa, after the Saab disaster I will be sticking with Japanese-a).

8. People really use their bodies here. Not wrapped in 20 denier, control top, reinforced toe, ultra sheer hosiery and other such finery, manicured and pedicured and pro-tected from the environment, but really used!

9. Beautiful women with long, slender necks (a neck like I want instead of the pudgy, consumption-slackened jawline that I have) and handsome men with sinewy, muscled bodies. To see them is to understand why they win marathon races.

10. The plethora of Michael Bolton Concert Tour and Titanic: The Movie t-shirts — it makes me chuckle.

Well, I'm off to run errands today, pick up my pass-port, go to the pharmacy, etc. (my EarNoseThroat doctor gave me these wonderful cortisone-based ear drops to take with in case of infection and I've discovered that they work absolute miracles on the cuts on my legs and the heat rashes on my face and neck as well! A rather multi-purpose application, must find more!).

One other thing I love about the music and dancing here is that it makes it okay for me to sing and dance all over the place too and nobody even looks twice!! Well, okay, I don't usually dance because in the company of Africans, everybody knows that white girls can't dance, but I rather enjoy cruising down the street chiming in with the ubiquitous Bob Marley — "Get up, stand up! Stand up for your rights!" Yeah, baby.

My hour is up again and I must go! Hope all is well in all the corners of the earth that you may habitate,

The last e-mail from Bamako,
Laura xoxo

# Chapter 15
# A Letter to the Premier

9 June 2001: Bobo-Dioulasso, Burkina Faso

Laura Enridge
Bobo-Dioulasso
Burkina Faso

June 9, 2001

Premier Gordon Campbell
Province of British Columbia
House of Parliament
Victoria, B.C.

Dear Mr. Premier,

May I call you Gord-o?

Congratulations on your recent election victory. Had I been there, I would have voted for you, as there really wasn't anybody any stinkin' better.

If you remember, your predecessor received quite a bit of heat over choosing to expand the SkyTrain line as the means for broadening Greater Vancouver's public transit. Having been in West Africa for a few months now, I have experienced some alternate means and have come up with a few suggestions which might prove useful in the future.

1. Bull-drawn carriage — Quite the hardy animal, the bull can negotiate a variety of terrains. A couple of wheels and some planks thrown together on the back and you've got room for 5, possibly 6 people plus cargo. The bull is prompted into action by applying pressure to his testicles, most effectively done with shoes removed. This method may even come quite easily to you, in fact, as I'm sure you've kicked a few people in the balls in years past.

2. Bachés, tro-tros and woro-woros — All are similar in nature — minivans or kombis or pickup trucks with bench seating added to the flatbed. Really quite efficient as they can achieve great speeds, and while they may only have seating for 12 or 14, can really accommodate up to 20 people. I'm sure folks won't object to being cosy on a cold winter's day. Translink may have to provide a bit stricter regulation, though, on things which don't seem to matter much here, such as working windshield wipers, the existence of windows, and lug nuts on the tires.

3. Mobylettes — Better known to us as the moped. Easy to park, doesn't need an extra vehicle lane, and

extremely fuel efficient. Drawbacks: bruising of the buttocks when riding shotgun without a seat cushion, and prone to flat tires at some point on most journeys, as I experienced in the 10 km stretch of no-man's land between the C'ote d'Ivoire and Mali frontiers, 35 minutes before border closing. Selling points: large women can ride them in skirts, dresses and other regalia.

I hope this comes in handy when your new administration is planning for the future. "Why reinvent the wheel?" I always say.

Sincerely,
Laura Enridge

P.S. Please keep Christy Clark's media sound bites to a minimum.

# Chapter 16
# The Mosquitos are as Persistent as the People

10 June 2001: Bobo-Dioulasso, Burkina Faso

Hi all,

How are things? I have arrived in Burkina Faso, and am currently in Bobo, due to leave for Ouagadougou shortly. This is a nice little town, not too hot, not too crowded, not too noisy, but MAN, can a person ever get hassled here. First there are the souvenir hawkers, who come after you at every turn. I find myself getting very rude and abrupt with them, and haven't yet mastered the sweet and docile brush-off. Then I find myself not liking who I become after an afternoon of hassles. It's a catch-22. There is a nice hotel here, about a three-star, and non-guests can pay to use the pool, so I've spent a couple of afternoons in there because it is tranquil and nobody can get to me!! Second, there are the mosquitos here, whose tenacity matches the inhabitants of this town. They are ruthless! Even when I am slathered in repellent, have a fan going, and a mosquito coil burning. And they even bite during the day, which they're not technically supposed to (I don't know why, but it has worked in every other place). So I've been a bit scratchy lately.

I was in the bank the day I got here and met a woman from Vancouver whilst cashing travellers cheques. She is on a traveling vacation, but also picked up a contract from the UBC Museum of Anthropology to purchase textiles whilst here. So we've been hanging out a bit and are going to head to Gorom-Gorom together on Wednesday for their apparently out-of-this world market which happens every Thursday. It's a seven hour bus ride each way so it better be a good market! I have my heart set on buying a Tuareg-made leather box. The Tuareg are the nomadic people of the Sahara who now live in some towns in Mali and Burkina. They are very different looking from other Africans as they descend from the Moroccan Berbers, and they usually wear indigo robes which turns their skin blue, but apparently they like that. Anyway, they make these fantastically beautiful leather boxes, so I am going in search of one.

Mali was such an interesting country once I got into the small towns, but it was just oh-so-hot that I had to get out (40 plus degrees). I spent three days trekking in Dogon Country, where the Tellem pygmy people built these freaky little houses into the middle of the cliff in the 12th century and got up and down by using pulley ropes. Now all these small traditional mud architecture villages have cropped up at the base of and on top of this breathtaking red sandstone escarpment, so each day I'd walk about six to 11 kms from village to village and then spend the night sleeping on the roof of the chief's house.

It is tradition to give him a gift of cola nuts, which are the nuts that were originally used in Coca Cola, where the coca was cocaine and this stuff was the other half and is also a mild hallucinogenic, apparently. Give them one nut and they think you're really nice, give them 3 or 4 and they think you're a goddess! Anyway, it was really fantastic. I was accompanied by a local guide and he knew so much about the history of the region as his father had done guiding through there for 30 years as well, so it was really great.

Also went to Mopti and Djenne, very old, very traditional towns along the River Niger. Djenne has the biggest mud brick building in the world in its mosque. It was really a completely different Africa than I am used to. Am regrouping in Bobo, as in having a shower that isn't just a bucket of water and a cup and actually being able to do laundry etc. Don't plan to spend much time in Burkina, as there are many things I want to do in Togo, so I'm budgeting my time for that. The weeks are counting down!!

Some specifics:

Dad — e-mails to Sharyn are bouncing, so the address I've got isn't correct.

Val and Nick — congrats on the house purchase in Vernon, that's big news!

Karen — yes, I can help you decorate on the Friday night before the wedding.

Sis — how'd you survive B's 40th?

Stacey and Arlene — be persistent with the antibiotic cream or your bellybuttons will get infected and you'll have to abort the mission.

Marion — yes, they do eat monkeys out here, and cats and dogs too.

Keep well, all! Talk to you soon,
Laura xoxox

# Chapter 17
# Rural is Rural

Truthfully, when I landed in Africa, a visit to Mali wasn't even on my agenda. I'd never heard of Sahel architecture or the Falaise de Bandiagara, and I'd forgotten that there really is a town called Timbuktu, and Mali is where it is found. My guidebook gave glowing descriptions of the country, however, calling it the "gem of West Africa, and the English VSO volunteers that I'd met in Ghana said that they were all planning to go there when their contracts ended. Eventually, when I did land up in Bamako and started a route along the River Niger, the things that I saw made me feel like I had stumbled onto something timeless, rare and utterly mysterious. I was incredibly thankful that I'd made the decision to go.

The first upriver stop that I made was in Mopti. I found it to be a rather strange town. It had an air of desperation, like an old man gasping for his last few breaths, clutching your hand with every ounce of strength he has left. In Bamako, I had been able to pretty much come and go wherever I wanted in the city without being bothered. The tour guides, money changers and souvenir hawkers wouldn't leave me alone for even a second in Mopti.

I was staying in a private house with Petra and Roland, the couple that I'd met on the night bus on the way up. Much to our chagrin, the owners were even letting guides come right into our room to try and talk us into taking a tour of the city, or hiring them to go into Dogon Country. We could barely get them out again once they had crossed the threshold of our doorway! One such guide followed me as I left the house to walk down the street towards the center of town. He nattered at me incessantly, and I tried to ignore him. It wasn't the response he desired, I guess, because he started yelling and screaming, saying that I had told him to fuck off, that he was going to call the police, and that I was in big trouble. Interesting sales tactic. Anyway, I had said no such thing to him, but it was still rather unnerving having him dog me all the way to the end of the road. He even stopped to talk with the policeman on one of the corners, at which point I kept right on walking and disappeared around a corner and into a shop to hide out for a few minutes. It wasn't pleasant.

There were a few things that I enjoyed about Mopti. One was watching the pirogues and pinasses floating down the River Niger, loaded down with sheep, goats (I could never tell which was which), people and cargo. It made for a spectacular scene against the setting sun. The other thing was hanging out with Petra and Roland, a very interesting couple. She was German, he was from England, and they were planning a future full of trips together.

West Africa was at the top of the list, and they had come over with ten weeks to travel first through Senegal, then Mali, Burkina Faso, and Ghana.

Upon their arrival in Dakar, they'd hooked up with a fellow in the street that had offered them cheap accommodation. Nothing too unusual about that; it happened all the time. The days and weeks that followed, however, were, by the sounds of it, completely bizarre.

Roland characterized this Senagalese guy as very charismatic, and said that in the first couple of days of staying at his property, he'd entertained him with man-to-man stories about his own virility, the power of the mind, and how he could get any woman he desired. The proof seemed to be in the pudding, because over the next while, both Petra and Roland saw him in the company of many a female, at varying stages of undress. He then gave Petra and Roland the gift of a beautiful drum, which they kept in their room with them. He also cooked their meals, quite eagerly, in fact, according to Roland.

Originally, they had planned on staying in Dakar for about five nights. They already had all of their visas for the other countries, and were excited to embark on the route that they'd planned out ahead of time. Five nights turned into ten, however, then ten into fifteen. After twenty-five nights, Roland and Petra finally got out of Dakar, half of their trip wasted in just one city.

So what kept them there? Amazingly, neither of them could tell me. Petra said that they would talk about leaving, saying, "Okay, tomorrow, we are moving on. Tomorrow, we have to move on." But tomorrow would come and go, and they would still be there. Physically, they both felt weaker than normal. Mentally, they were unclear and unfocused. Outwardly, they weren't showing any signs of actual illness, though. Their gracious host kept telling them that he did not want them to depart, that his place was the place where they should be. And even though they both wanted to go, they just couldn't get away. It took them five weeks!

As they told me this strange story, it was clear that both Petra and Roland were extremely troubled and upset by the ordeal. As a result of it, their schedule had been compressed to such a degree that they had to skip Burkina Faso and parts of Ghana. They were even more concerned by the fact that they had to leave the continent via Dakar at the end of the trip. They really didn't want to go anywhere near this freaky guy again, feeling lucky for just having been able to get away from him at all.

To them, the only explanation for the whole chain of events was that he had put them under a spell. Having visited a fetish market or two along the way in West Africa, I can't say I disagree with their hypothesis. They've got the stuff to whip up any number of potions, that's for sure. And while voodoo in Africa is generally practiced as a spirituality that provides elements of good, its spirits can also be called upon for malevolent practices. Why the unsuspecting pair of Petra and Roland might have been chosen as the targets for somebody's bad juju is anybody's guess. It was the closest I'd ever come to a voodoo 'incident,' and the story left me just a tiny bit spooked for the two days that I hung out with them in Mopti.

One of the most visually and spiritually amazing things that a traveller can do in Mali is trek through the vast and open expanses of Dogon Country, along the Falaise. I went to the town of Bandi-agara exactly for that reason: to hire a guide, buy supplies, and be in starting proximity to one of the villages along the escarpment. My plan was to spend two nights and three days out in the open desert. I had heard the trekking was brutally hard on your body — rising at dawn each morning, walking for two or three hours, rest-ing through the heat of the day, and then walking that much again — so I didn't think I'd be able to survive much more than a few days.

Although quickly befriended by a scrawny, red-eyed guide upon my arrival in town, I heard from a couple of locals that his tendency was to drink all night and then not want to get up and start the walk in the morning. I opted instead to hire Mamadou, who came from a well-established Malian family (his father had owned the hotel in which I was staying, and had guided in the region for 30 years. He had passed away while in his early 50s, not unusual for Africa). I signed a hand-written contract that Mama-dou and I had written up together, however the transaction was not completed without a rousing argument between him and the party-prone guide. (He felt that Mamadou had pushed him aside,

A taxi driver in Accra transports a woman and her mountain of mangoes.

Fishing boats line the shore of the Atlantic at Kokrobite, Ghana.

Cape Coast Castle, a former slave fort in Ghana, is now a UNESCO World Heritage site.

Martha, at left, is the daughter of the man credited with starting the Boabeng-Fiema Monkey Sanctuary in Ghana.

Women hurriedly sell bread and hard-boiled eggs to passengers on my bus as we pull out of the Abidjan depot.

I posed with Beah, the owner of this Sassandra restaurant, before digging into a delicacy called *crab facil*.

In a village in western Côte d'Ivoire, my guide Mikhael takes me to watch women perform the arduous task of pounding grain to make *foutou*.

A stilt dancer shows off his skills in a performance that was arranged for my enjoyment in western Côte d'Ivoire.

*La Dent de Man*, the Tooth of Man, in Côte d'Ivoire.

I could have done a whole series of photos on people sleeping in odd places. This one was in Bamako, Mali.

Foosball is a popular pastime in Bamako. Tables can be found on sidewalks, in open lots and cafés.

Local women trading at the daily market in Mopti, Mali. Colourful prints are focal in the dress of West Africans.

A pirogue drifts down the River Niger at dusk in Mali, loaded with a cargo of people, animals and goods.

The *togu-na* is where elders meet to discuss village matters in Dogon Country, Mali.

At the twice-weekly market in Bandiagara, a woman sells dried beans, while next to her some donkeys wait to begin the long walk home.

A large tree stands out against the stark landscape of Dogon Country, Mali.

The 12th-Century pygmy houses in Dogon Country are built in the middle section of a tall rock escarpment.

The door of a house in Dogon Country, Mali. Door carvings like these are a common sight in this region of the country.

Rather than wait for the ferry across the River Niger at Djenné, the driver of my bush taxi opted to drive across the river.

This mud-brick mosque in Djenné, Mali, is the largest mud structure in the world.

Beautiful multi-coloured windows are a common part of the
Sahel mud-brick architecture in Djenné, Mali.

Stuck in no-man's land: our moped gets a flat while transiting between borders.

An unconventional method for transporting raw meat in Mali: some men tie a side of beef to the roof rack of our vehicle.

Women of the Fula tribe discuss matters on the main street in Gorom-Gorom, Burkina Faso.

A man cuts a dashing figure as he rides away from a camel trade in Gorom-Gorom, Burkina Faso.

Oku (front and centre), my drum teacher in Kokrobite, Ghana, performs with a group for travelers at a local beach resort.

which, in fact, was not too far from the truth. I had observed a little jostling between them from the window of my second floor room).

When morning arrived, I went out to the street to wait for my guide. He arrived on a moped, the best (and most cost effective) mode of transport that he could arrange. We only needed it for the first leg, to get ourselves out to the starting point of our trek, but as I climbed on, I noticed with dismay that this particular moped was minus a seat cushion on the back. This wouldn't have been quite so bad if it was just me sans gear and we were on graded roads, but I was weighed down by my pack and the ruts and potholes were many. After an hour, it felt like all the flesh on my respectably-padded butt had reached wafer-thin compression, and I was riding bone-on-metal. The pain was excruciating, but I didn't want Mamadou to think me a wimp; after all, we hadn't even started the trekking yet. We stopped once so I could "readjust my pack" (a thinly-veiled excuse) and eventually arrived at our destination around 11 a.m.

Over those three days, we visited a total of seven villages. Some were high atop the escarpment, some were nestled at its base. They weren't radically different from each other, but they were a world away from the consumerism that has reached even African cities like Bamako. Aside from seeing the occasional plastic wrapper from some digestive cookies that had been tossed on the ground (about as fancy as it gets in the local cookie-making industry), there wasn't very much to indicate in which decade, or even century, we were in. I think that if I had brought up some example of current world events in conversation, I would have been met by blank stares. The activities that took place on an average day in these villages were probably no different than what would have happened 400 years ago, or what was happening 50 years ago.

A manifestation of this, I noticed, was that the people of Dogon, (especially the women), would expend a great deal of energy each day just ensuring that basic needs were met. Drawing water from the well, hand-washing clothes, pounding grain, working in the fields, and cooking were the tasks that would essentially use up all the hours of light that were available in one day. If anybody had any additional time to work on anything else, say a side project of weaving baskets or whatever, I do not know where they would have found the energy.

And then there was market day. Once a week, one of the villages in the region would set up for a day of trading wares; sad, little tomatoes, grains, dried onion balls, okra, and an assortment of household items that had been hauled in from the nearest town. People walked 20 kilometres to get to these markets, dragging with them the goods they aimed to sell, and then walked 20 kilometres home again, new purchases in tow. It all seemed so incredibly futile (and difficult) to me, but it was business as usual for them.

In contrast, here at home we actually pay to take courses on time management just to ensure that we get the right balance of work and play in our daily lives! We have to make choices about which gyms to join, which ski resorts to buy our seasons lift passes for, early show or late show, Thai or Indian food on Friday night? The options are endless, the pleasures plentiful. Even when we're at work, we play. Latté breaks in the morning to catch up on last weekend's gossip, lunches spent at the driving range, perhaps. We have time, and we have disposable income (some more than others, but we can generally all afford to rent a video or DVD to play on our in-home, hi-fi, surround-sound, audio-visual systems). What do people in a rural village in Africa do for fun?

It is a question I don't think I can even answer. I don't recall ever really seeing someone having what we'd normally refer to as fun. Sitting around talking with each other in the evening, sure. Sure, that's nice, but I wouldn't call it sensory stimulation! A few times, I witnessed a game of chess or another local board game played by some men. More often, though, what I saw was work all day, rest when it gets too hot, talk some at night, and then go to bed. No sign of books, no sign of toys, no sign of real sports equipment or hobby supplies or gear of any sort. I used to wonder if the villagers realized that their existence was rather sombre. But did they feel they were missing out on something? Did they bemoan a life without amusement parks, casinos and ski resorts? Or did they find their joy in just seeing the sun rise faithfully each morning?

For some reason, it made me happy when I noticed that there was evidence of traditional arts in all of the villages that I visited (it was a peculiar emotional response, I thought, because I normally hadn't given even that much thought to the upholding of the First Nations' artistic legacy in my own country). I'm not sure if these skills — weaving, wood carving, mud cloth painting, dancing, etc. — are taught in at least some small part in the majority of families, or if they are passed down through an artisan group (I suspect the latter). At any rate, the products of these trades were not only created to sell to tourists such as myself (although supply definitely exceeded demand in that respect), but were also in use throughout the communities. People wore hand-woven and indigo-dyed clothing, and hung the most fantastically carved doors on their otherwise functionally-designed mud houses. As for performing arts, Mamadou told me that the event of harvesting the crops was cause for a great celebration that brought on days' worth of singing and dancing. I can only imagine what a ceremony for marriage or death would entail.

It may be that the combination of traditional ceremonies and festivals, mixed in with the odd game of barefoot soccer (the ball being made of anything at all that could be taped up into a round object), provided enough leisure-time activities to keep most folks pretty content. Happiness does not necessarily take the form of a video game or a concert ticket, and sometimes when it does, it is at the expense of some of the simpler, (yet still beautiful, and most definitely valuable), things around us that could be part of our lives. For people such as the Dogon of Mali, living miles away from the consumer marketplaces of the cities has actually helped them retain some of the things in their lives that otherwise may have been lost through time.

Not having grown up in rural Africa, I would never presume that what we have in the West is what they should also aspire to achieve on their continent. What I wish for them, however, is that eventually they are able to attain some of the things that we have enjoyed here for several generations: primary health care, access to education, food security, and personal safety. I hope that one day they don't have to work so hard just to provide one or two meals a day for their families, that things come a little easier to them. I hope that they continue to allow themselves to be guided by their culture and their spirituality, rather than by trends and markets. And I hope that this is enough to create their happiness, they that are thousands of miles across the world, down quiet, dusty roads, living in clusters of mud-brick huts. From what I have seen, I think it will be.

# Chapter 18
# Sleeping on Rooftops

The fine art of sleeping is something that I see as highly undervalued in Western society. Debased, even. The people who liberally partake in slumber are often thought of as lazy, sloth-like and self-indulgent. Say what? I am not a sloth, sir, I am a human being. And I love to nap. I'm a proud napper, in fact. I can put my cheek down on my desk at work and be at the fluttering eyelid stage within ten minutes if the mood is right and the phone doesn't ring.

After years of fighting some strange internal guilt over this, I have finally come to accept the fact that dissimilar metabolisms and different climates require varying amounts of rest. Just because my co-worker functions just fine on six hours a night and can show up all perky and energetic at eight a.m. does not mean that there is something wrong with me if I can't. (Which I can't). If left undisturbed, my normal nightly doze is ten hours. And now, when I go to work on Monday morning and someone asks me, "So, what did you get up to this weekend?" I know that there is absolutely nothing wrong with responding to that question with "Nothin' really. Slept a bunch."

That said, may I now crown myself the undisputed Queen of Sleep? (Or perhaps Goddess of Sleep. I like the sound of that better). Friends, family and people afar have marveled at my abilities. The drop-and-doze technique has been particularly useful in all my years of traveling. There was the all-nighter that a friend and I pulled in the Athens airport when we were 18, for one. I got a good three hours of shut-eye in while she sat bored and fidgety, annoyed with me for not keeping her company. It probably didn't help her that we had parked ourselves and our gear off to one side of a cement staircase. For me, all it meant was that I awoke with a dandy pattern of stair-edge impressions up and down my body.

Had I been more on the ball when I was traveling through West Africa, I would have done a whole, gorgeous series of portraits on sleep and people in the midst of it. The sheer variety of places that I saw eyes fully shut would have been worthy of at least five or six pages of photos. It was completely impressive.

If a car was neatly parked under a shady tree, then its hood might become a lounge for the weary. A market vendor was really only expected to be awake and selling for half the day, it seemed. The other half was choice napping time, and well deserved at that, as the day often began at six a.m. If a young man was out in the street pushing his cart along and happened to fall tired, then his cart would double as a cot. The possibilities were endless. Chairs, benches, shop-front floors, middles of parks, edges of parks, next to parks — endless! And everybody did it, so nobody looked out of place. Truck drivers would lay in the shade underneath their trucks, taxi drivers lounged in friendly clusters of two or three next to a cold drink stand. The normal, noisy activities of the day could be going on all around, and still, people would sleep. West Africans obviously recognized the value of a good nap.

At night, sleeping was often a group event. Forget about the private room, you matted down with at least one or two other members of your family, and it could very well be a multi-generational cross-section: grandma, husband and wife, and child. Being the practical person that I am, I found this perplexing. When did the baby-making happen? I wondered. When did the baby-making happen? Obviously, it was happenin' somewhere!

To facilitate the function, some families chose the complete set of bed frame, box spring and mattress, while others, either because of cost or preference, slept on foam mats or blankets on the ground. Sometimes, it was a combination of both, such as the time when I was befriended while traveling on a tro-tro and stayed for a night with Augusta and her Aunty Peace in Akosombo, Ghana. One of the regular beds was given up for me. Augusta still stayed in the same room, but took the floor, as did her brother's girlfriend. I felt somewhat guilty, but she assured me that she actually preferred that over the soft and lumpy old mattress. It showed me that having a measure of wealth in Africa didn't always change old habits.

Sometimes, people just slept any old place. More than once, I'd get up in the middle of the night to go to the toilet and practically trip over a body or two sprawled out near the entrance. It wouldn't have been my first pick for a spot, but there's no accounting for taste (or smell, in that instance). Finally, for those who preferred elevation off the ground but couldn't afford a store-bought version, there was what I call the Super Weave: very bendy-flexy plant materials tightly interlaced to form a hammock-like mattress, which was then suspended from sturdy tree-branch bed legs. I only ever saw these in singles, and imagine that while working up a double or queen size would be nice, it wouldn't be the most sound structure for gettin' busy on. And since snuggling in 40-plus weather would be the equivalent of hugging a lifesized hot water bottle while already in the throes of a fever, the labour expended on building the bigger bed would have only gone to waste.

The conversion of rooftops into sleeping areas was hands-down one of the most brilliant uses of space I'd ever seen. With temperatures reaching the highs that they do in the arid deserts of Africa, architecture obviously had to respond. As a result, mud-brick homes are built with these great, flat roofs, and they are utilized as everyday living space. Even when sleeping on the roof, though, you'd likely be sharing the space with several others. Everybody would drag their mats up the tree-branch carved ladder and throw them down to claim their spot. Sometimes there'd be an animal or two, sometimes even a cooking fire if dinner was running late. It was yet another kind of group lounging experience, and so much more enchanting with the carpet of stars to gaze up at while drifting off.

On a couple of occasions, I was lucky enough to have a roof-top to myself. Once it was while I was in Bandiagara, Mali. I had rented a hotel room in a rather popular establishment, but there didn't seem to be any other guests around at the time. The cleaning man showed me the staircase, precariously steep and with steps that only supported a small portion of my foot, and suggested that I take a mat up there that night. Later, after using up about 30 minutes having dinner in the center of town, I was bored. I hadn't found a place where I was comfortable to sit and hang out for a while, and I hadn't come across any books written in English since forever. I came back to the hotel, brushed my teeth, and pulled a mattress from a spare bed that was, likely permanently, located in the open area outside my room.

I half expected that the cleaning man would be showing up there later, too, as many hotel staff live on-site 24/7. He didn't, though, so it was just me and a big, wide open space. I spent a couple of hours just listening to the night and staring up at the sky. There was a lovely breeze, just enough that it didn't blow the dirt from the roof into my eyes and mouth, which had happened other nights on other roofs. The sky had a pink glow for the first while, until it became very dark, and then I could see all the stars. It was almost completely quiet, and aside from hearing snippets of conversations here and there, the noises were all sounds of the night. I felt very small and very far away from home, and I could hardly believe it that I was even there at all. It was wonderful.

Often, privacy isn't the only challenge that one is faced with after-hours. Luckily, Africans seem to have developed the ability to remain semi-conscious through noises that fall only slightly short of a complete Armageddon. There are the discos, for one. They're everywhere, because all it takes to be a disco in Africa is some chairs and a stereo. If there is any such thing as noise by-laws, they aren't enforced. Oh no, these babies keep cranking until the wee, small hours of the morn. Then, there are the dueling discos. That's when they open shop right next door to each other. One will play its utterly horrible 1970s B-sides cassette over and over again, and the other will play Celine Dion all night, which is equally utterly horrible, really.

Under normal circumstances, I wouldn't have found this a problem. At home, I can sleep through fire alarms and car thieves hack-sawing their way into my underground garage. The temperature factor, though, kept me awake on those nights in Africa, sweating and miserable in a small, claustrophobic room, swatting at buzzing mosquitoes, flailing about for hours until exhaustion would eventually give way to slumber, usually at about four in the morning. Those were the places where I only stayed for one night and modified my route in order to get away, if need be.

In addition to discos, there are also the distressed roosters. These are the somewhat confused birds that don't confine their crowing only to the break of day; rather, they never actually stop crowing through any of the a.m. hours. They are everywhere, cities and villages, and seemingly in the backyard of every structure next to the one you're staying in. Finally, there is the fundamental lack of building insulation. PinkPak just has no place in that part of the world. I mean, sometimes walls don't even go all the way up to meet ceilings, and just how tight can you really weave a thatched roof, anyway? Even if you are in a cement hotel, you have to keep the windows open for some air, so there's no soundproofing achieved there, either.

Getting a good, uninterrupted sleep was something that I placed great value on during my travels through West Africa, right alongside the acquisition of drinkable water and the location of decent toilet facilities. It was a constant challenge, but one that I met head on (or face down, rather), being the trooper that I am. On some nights, I did better than others (and on some mornings, I was decidedly less bitchy than on others as a result). Whatever the case, I faced each day with the comfort of knowing that in another 15 hours or so, I'd get to try it all over again.

# Chapter 19
# Oh, and Rodents, Too...

**12 June 2001: Ouagadougou, Burkina Faso**

Can't forget to mention that they eat rodents, too. On one of my many kombi journeys I was riding along feeling like a little princess because I had scored the coveted front seat next to the driver, until we hit a pothole and the glove box popped open into my lap and lo and behold there was the biggest, deadest mofo of a rat laying inside!! I, of course, screamed but nobody else even batted a single naturally-curly African eyelash. It was the driver's dinner.

Yesterday's bus ride from Bobo to Ouaga was much more pleasant. About a half hour into it, I was just hitting that relaxed sleepy state when something very alive brushed up against my feet. I started and then bent down into the aisle to look under my seat and the man behind me said, "Pardon, c'est mon coq," that being of the type that crows every morning at the break of dawn (well, I guess they both do but anyway). So I had his coq tickling my ankles about every 20 minutes after that for 5 hours, but better than a rat, ja?

Anyway, gotta fly!! On the road to Gorom-Gorom tomorrow...

Ciao from Ouaga,
Laura xoxo

P.S. Sharon, please tell Tyler that I'M IN OUAGA-DOUGOU!!

P.P.S. I can't believe April is pregnant!!!!!!!!!!!!

# Chapter 20
# To Hell, Via Gorom-Gorom

Hi all, howzit? Thanks for all the e-mail news, positive words of support, etc. It is really a great thing to hear from your friends when you are traveling alone. I feel like I am missing out on a lot of stuff back home and am starting to look forward to coming back to good old Canada, believe it or not. Africa, great as it is, can be hard on a person too!! Having ingested dust into every orifice possible over the last couple of weeks in the desert, I am suffering yet another sinus infection coupled with an ear infection as a result of my dust allergy not liking it too much, so I've been a tired soul lately!!

The trip to Gorom-Gorom was oh so difficult. First, it is a looooong way away — right up in the top north east of Burkina, near the Niger and Mali borders. Second, it is hot hot hot, sitting right on the edge of the Sahara desert. The TV news said 42 degrees but I think it was hotter!! Third, dusty. Couldn't keep the dust out of anything, and it's a yicky feeling when you're hot and covered in dust. I couldn't imagine how the people live up there; it is such an unforgiving environment.

I went with Michelle, the Canadian girl I mentioned, and there were also four English on the bus that I'd met in Mali, so there was quite the tourist contingent for a change. We stayed in a town called Dori because there were rooms with air-conditioning there, and then had to commute on market day to Gorom, about 50 kms away. The transport was the worst yet that I've taken here in Africa, and I've taken some bad ones. I don't know if it is because it is such an outpost that there is no medical around for people or what, but it felt like the truck was being driven by the grim reaper, I'm telling you. Next to me was a boy of about 10, sitting there with raw, bleeding, fly-attracting, festering elbows, which he would bump me with every now and then. I got so nauseous from this (and worried that I'd pick something up from him) that I asked to switch places and ended up sitting on the spare tire with a rim jamming into me. There was also a woman and her baby with a really bad case of conjunctivitis. Ick. And a couple of children that I kid you not, looked to be on the verge of death. It was one of the saddest cases of inhumanity I've ever seen, and nobody has any rights at all to say, hey, quit jamming those extra three people in on top of me. They just suffer, crammed in like cattle, even worse. Michelle and I barely made it, we were pretty shaken up by the whole thing.

Gorom itself was actually disappointing. I'd seen better and more fun markets in Mali, so I was quite let down, having traveled all that distance. But it was interesting, still, with camel traders and Tuareg men and Fula women with rows of silver hoops hanging from their hair and ears. The tricky part is getting photos of these people without offending them!! I didn't find the multi-coloured leather box I was looking for, so I guess short of going back to Mali I'm SOL!! But I just bought a beautiful one-colour leather Tuareg box here in Ouaga, so all is not lost in the shopping expedition.

I'm going to see some live music tonight at an outdoor garden type club — people playing the kora, which is a funky cross between a guitar and a harp. Tomorrow I'm off to Togo for about a week to 10 days, and then back into Ghana for the last little bit before coming home.

I found out some interesting stuff about Côte d'Ivoire since being there. Apparently the President of C.D. that was just elected last October has been traveling around West Africa trying to save face because they have been finding many many many shallow graves around the country in C.D. Remember when I said there are lots of police roadblocks and we would always lose one or two people who didn't have proper papers? Well the people without papers are either Burkinabes or Malian, and apparently Côte d'Ivoire doesn't want them there, so they have been torturing and killing them in an effort to start a genocide scare and get them to all go back home. Nice, hey? So those people that get pulled off the buses could be in for a number of fates. It is frightening to consider.

The inter-regional migration is the crux of many problems though, in this area. ECOWAS, the Economic Community of West African States, was formed to parallel the EC in some ways, and allow the free trade of goods and the free movement of labour. So labour has been moving alright, but it isn't going as smoothly as it should because of the degree of police and military corruption and lawlessness.

Anyway, I should go and shower as I worked up a real sweat bargaining with the dudes in the market for my box!! Keep the news coming as it is psyching me up for my return home. I've been pondering the situation of the B.C. parliament — what kind of a sham is that going to be if the Liberals have all but two seats? Any politico-analyst input? (I nominate Scott T.).

Catch y'all soon!
Love Laura xoxoxox

# Chapter 21
# The Lost Girls

The days when I had a traveling companion in West Africa were few and far between. I didn't run into many tourists on my route, and when I did, they were usually Japanese — friendly enough, but still not of my native tongue. Finding an English-speaking, slang-flinging Westerner was a blessing. Finding one from your own hometown was nothing short of a small miracle.

I was having an extraordinarily difficult time cashing some traveler's cheques in a bank in Bobo-Dioulasso. As it happened, my American Express cheques didn't look exactly like the sample American Express cheque that was taped up to the teller's window. The cheque displayed through the glass was in Euros, and since mine was different, this quietly stubborn woman was convinced that her place of employ didn't accept it. I made every effort to get her to move beyond the linear and apply logic to the situation.

My frustration was growing, but I was trying hard to suppress my smartass trigger and keep her on my side, knowing that she was the one with the cash. Eventually, having been essentially dismissed by the shrug of her shoulders, I gave up and escalated the issue to the bank manager. Inside his office, I retold my story. For this pain, I received prompt and courteous customer service, worthy of a Wall Street financial institution, and my transaction was completed. It was at that moment that a disheveled and unhealthy-looking white girl walked in the door and toward the teller's window.

My first instinct was to warn her of the impending difficulty that she faced if she was planning on cashing traveler's cheques. Once I'd told her how to get around that little hurdle, we started talking routes — where she'd come from, where I was going, when we were going home. As it turned out, for us, home was the same place.

Michelle originally came from Saskatoon, but had been living in Vancouver for almost two years. It seemed to me that she was equally happy to find a kindred that day, and it didn't take long for her to ramble into the story of how a girl could stay just that white while in Africa. Today, she explained, was the first day that she had walked — physically taken steps — in three days.

While traveling from Ghana to Burkina Faso with a Ghanaian friend, she had come down with malaria. Lucky to have someone watch over her, she had spent those three days fading in and out of consciousness in a hospital bed, hoping that the nurses were using clean needles each time they changed her intravenous.

Now she was back on the road, taking things slowly, but incredibly thankful to have come through the worst of what can only be described as an ordeal. In comparison, all those times that I'd had to wait hours and hours for transportation, those were inconveniences. Getting dumped on the side of the road in San-sanné-Mango, a mile out of town, at an hour before midnight, that was unsafe and a right pain in the ass. Coming down with malaria in Africa, though, is the worst fear of every traveler, and a true test of their spirit. Michelle had come through it with flying colours. She was brimming with stories of her adventures, and it was obvious that she had the same love of the region as I. A friendship was formed then, not only out of desperation for companionship, but also from our common passion for life in faraway places. And for a brief few days in Burkina Faso, we lived it together.

Aside from the Booby Market grocery, Bobo-Dioulasso was not the most interesting of places I'd been to in West Africa, so after a few days, I decided to leave for the capital city of Ouaga-dougou. Michelle and I had both expressed an interest in taking a trip from there up to Gorom-Gorom, in the northeast corner of the country. It seemed like a horribly long haul just to go and experience it's famous Thursday market, but from all the accounts we'd heard, it was an incomparable sight. If her and I could some-how tag up again in Ouaga and synchronize our transport up there, it would at least make the trip sufferable. We were just going to have to play it by ear.

I completed all my schedule arrangements once I got back to the capital city and was all set to go. There were two different bus companies that piloted the road from Ouaga to Gorom-Gorom, and since Michelle and I had parted ways in Bobo, it was with pure joy that I saw her waiting at the bus station, my bus station, at 7:30 a.m. that Wednesday morning. We found no shortage of things to talk about for the duration of the drive, six-and-a-half hours, and the joy that came from sharing a girl-to-girl connection made us oblivious to the red desert dust that was flying in the windows and insidiously coating our skin, our bags, even getting into our ears. It was just a small sign of what was still to come.

With all the accommodation choices (three) located in the town of Dori, that's where we disembarked from the bus, stepping into a brick wall of heat. My body was overwhelmed by instant lethargy. I didn't think I was actually going to be able to walk, and upon trying, was convinced that our map was horribly out of scale and what said one kilometre was really ten. Once we found the lone hotel with reliable air conditioning, the rest of the day was spent doing as little as possible, as even being outside was nearly unbearable.

There's no doubt in my mind that I would have enjoyed the market at Gorom-Gorom a heck of a lot more if it hadn't been 45 degrees out that day. Very important note to self: do not go back to West Africa in the June-July time frame. A hotter place there could not have been. It was really difficult to savour the atmosphere when all I wanted to do was go find a shady place to sit and drink another soda (I think I consumed a record six that morning, plus 3 litres of water).

We spent a total of only about an hour out in the stalls, buying jewelry and searching for the elusive Tuareg multi-coloured leather box that I'd first seen in Mali and had coveted ever since. Although it once again evaded me, there was a grand display of sea foam green moulded plastic sneakers strung up at one of the booths. I reckoned there must have been a manufacturing over-supply in China at one point and someone in Burkina somehow struck a cheap import deal because, gawd, these shoes were on everyone's feet.

Personally, I would have desired a slightly more breathable footwear in that climate, but for the Burkinabe's, I guess the price was right. Worn as slip-ons, sans laces strung through the con-toured eyelets, they also came in ivory. Either colour could poten-tially glow in the dark, which could be quite a handy thing, really, when there weren't any street lamps to guide your safe passage and make sure you didn't bump into anybody in the night. You think I jest, but ever try walking around at night in Africa? All you see is the whites of their eyes in the moment before you have to veer to avoid collision.

Right in between the market and the shops that sold the sodas, a real live bus had pulled up and parked under a big tree. Michelle and I stopped to investigate, hopes high. Anything would've been better for the ride back to Dori than the manner in which we'd come. I honestly didn't think I could stomach another two-and-a-half hours in that wretched truck, stuffed in like cattle on the way to slaughter, our condition upon arrival of no consequence because we were just to be marched off to execution anyway. It had really felt that awful, no exaggeration. It horrified me that the locals traveled like that day in and day out.

Two men were sitting at a little table beside the bus, selling tickets. "Is it going back to Dori?" we asked. One of them told us that it was stopping in Dori and then continuing on to Ouaga. Michelle and I just looked at each other, wide-eyed. "How long does the bus stop for in Dori, sir?" "Half an hour," was his reply. Little lighbulbs went off in our heads. We could get out of this dustbowl and back to a balmy 40 degree climate tonight! We wouldn't have to stay another night in the desert! We explained to them that our bags were at the hotel in Dori, and asked if we ran all the way from the bus stop to collect them and then back again, would we have enough time before the bus continued on its way? "No problem," he assured us. We gleefully purchased tickets, not having thought the plan through enough to realize that we'd just committed to running a mile each way, fully-loaded with our gear for the second half of it.

It was now 11 a.m., and the bus didn't leave until one. Drunk from the heat, we stumbled back to a storefront and sat down to wait. My inertia brought on a wave of guilt. I had traveled such a long way to get to this town, and there I was, sitting on a step and drinking soda. At the back of my head, I knew there was much more to Gorom-Gorom than the sliver that I had glimpsed, but I was unable to move any further. The fact that Michelle was seemingly in as sad a shape as I provided a measure of comfort. We sat for two hours, watching the flow of people in their fantastic cotton prints and trying to surreptitiously take photos without raising anybody's ire.

When we boarded the bus at one o'clock, there were several other tourists already occupying the rows of red vinyl seats at the back, including the English that had been there on the way up. Between the bunches of us, we had been given three different departure times: one, two and three, which was fairly typical of the accuracy of transport scheduling in West Africa. It was well past the latter time before we saw any wheel movement at all, but we arrived in Dori in a fraction of the time that the morning commute had taken. Michelle and I were already in sprint position before the doors to the bus even opened, knowing that getting to the hotel and back in 30 minutes was going to be very tight. The bus employees assured us they would wait for us to return.

Amazingly, we really did run part of the way. I can't even imagine what we looked like. I know we felt like it was the most important mile of our lives. In the room, we were losing time on packing however, and as I frantically shoved things helter skelter into my backpack and tried to zip it shut, sweat dripped from my tomato-red face and onto the cordura fabric.

Michelle went out ahead of me to settle the bill, and by the time I got to the front of the hotel, she had found us a local fellow with a motor bike to ferry us one by one back to the bus. Oh, sweet Jesus, we'd been saved! I went first. The guy drove as quickly as he could through the sandy streets without completely fishtailing the bike and dumping us, and as he dropped me at the bus, I grabbed his shoulders and said excitedly, "Maintenant, mon amie! Maintenant, mon amie!" trying to convey the preciousness of every lost second. As he peeled off, I asked myself if I should have given him some money, then decided it was best to pay him upon completion of the task.

My happiness at being so close to getting out of northeastern Burkina quickly turned back to distress as first five minutes went by, then ten, then fifteen, and still no Michelle. The bus started to pull away. "Non, non, non! Attendez, s'il-vous plait!" I begged the bus driver. He assured me that he was only going 50 metres away to get gas, and then we would be stopping again. It was only around the corner, she'll still find us, I was thinking. Twenty minutes, no Michelle.

Venting to the other tourists, I peppered them with a series of unanswerable questions. "Did they have an accident? Did he not go back to get her? Is she hurt?" All the worst scenarios were flashing through my brain. The bus started its engine again. Now we were moving several hundred metres down the road to the police checkpoint at the outskirts of town. I stayed on the bus, fretting that she'd never be able to find us now, as we were beyond the sightline of the town centre. "What should I do?" Nobody responded. They didn't have to tell me that of course I should remain behind and find her. I badly wanted to stay on the bus and get out of Dodge. Pleading with the driver and the ticket man for five more minutes got me nowhere. "We can't wait for your friend any longer, sorry. We have to go. You can still use your ticket on tomorrow morning's bus."

Off they went. I gave a pathetic wave to the other backpackers as they looked down at me from the windows. Where was she? As I watched the bus roll away, belching diesel and kicking up dust, I started to cry. After all that effort, I knew that now I still had to walk all the way back to the hotel. Seeing that I was distraught, the policemen called me over to where they were set up under the tree. Wary, I explained my predicament, hoping that they would take pity on me and give me a lift. "We'll take you for 1500 cedis," they said. It was only a bit more than two dollars U.S., but indignant at the fact that the cops were trying to get cash out of me, I told them to forget it and stormed off. Forty-five minutes later, as I wandered lost through the sandy strips of street, I cried some more. Dumb, dumb, dumb, Laura! You should have taken the ride! I'd stop and ask for directions, but people would just vaguely point one way or another. Finally, after an hour, I found the hotel.

"What happened?" I asked the staff. "She walked," was all they could tell me. So what? I wondered, did she just get impatient and decide to hoof it and ended up screwing up the whole master plan? And where was she now? I stewed for a while. Hours had passed, and there was no sign of her. All of my charitable thoughts and concerns for her misfortune had vanished. By the time I'd gathered a couple of buckets of water for the shower and had my sponge off, though, she came back, springing through the door, clean, happy and seemingly unaffected by the fact that we'd missed the bus. Why was she not feeling as miserable as I was? I wondered.

The guy on the motor bike had never come back to get her. She'd waited and waited, and then deciding to make a last-ditch attempt at catching the bus, started walking. Her timing was such that she probably arrived less than 5 minutes after we'd pulled away from the gas station, right about the time that we were sitting at the police checkpoint. Realizing that she'd missed us, and then believing that I must have continued on with the bus, she angrily went to find a hotel that was closer than where we'd stayed the night before.

She'd showered, changed, and caught her breath before starting to rationalize that I could perhaps have actually gone back to the other room. Her decision to go look for me wasn't purely selfless; the air conditioning in her new digs was malfunctioning. That just would not do, so she grabbed her bags and left. Along the way, she'd met two very friendly folks that had bought her a Coke and given her a lift, so by the time she burst into the room in our original hotel, she didn't look like she'd been through half the battle that I had, and I was mildly aggravated.

Once we compared notes and I realized that she'd walked just as much as me, and had also cried, things were back to normal. We could not seem to figure out, though, why motorcycle dude had not come back to pick her up. He'd been all for helping us out at first. When he'd dropped me at the bus, we were as in-sync as a relay team in the 4x100 at the Olympics. What could have changed his path in the minutes afterwards?

As it turned out, Michelle had even run into him as she was walking dejectedly from the bus stop to the hotel. He'd sheepishly given her some lame excuse about needing to phone his wife, so that was why he couldn't live up to his commitment. "Are you kidding me?" she'd asked him, "you knew how much we needed to get on that bus!"

Maybe we should have been more clear in letting him know that there was some good money in it for him at the end, I don't know. At that point, all we could do was shake our heads and write it off to being yet another example of the way events transpire in Africa. We said a good half-dozen "ohmygod, I can't believe it" 's, had a laugh over it, and swore we'd be there waiting for the morning bus at least a half an hour ahead of time.

Africa just wanted to add insult to our injury, it seemed. The next day, about an hour into the trip back to Ouagadougou, somebody exited the bus via the back door and let loose the goat that was also in transit with us. There was a whole lot of yelling, and then the driver pulled over and parked. We sat and watched for an hour and a half while at least twelve men chased this bloody goat back and forth through the desert. They'd go one way, the goat would go the other. First the goat, then the stream of men, hands waving wildly in the air. They got so far away for a while that we couldn't even see them anymore. Michelle and I just looked at one another in disbelief over the fact that a bus in Burkina wouldn't wait even an extra ten minutes for a human being, but for a farm animal, well, the clock stopped ticking!

We were so affronted by this inversion of priorities that we quietly rooted for the goat and his quest for freedom. Eventually, the pursuants all returned to the bus, trophy in tow, and we were on our way again. A goat, after all, was worth six dollars! What were we worth? Clearly, as non-chattel, not as much as the goat.

# Chapter 22
# Who'da Thunk...?

20 June 2001: Lomé, Togo

....that I'd find a La Senza, Steve Madden etc. under-wear sale (most of them marked "Sample, Not for Sale") at the A-Plus Cash 'n Carry in Lome, Togo?? For fifty cents each?? I bought six pairs!!

Hi everyone! How are you? I'm a little less gloomy than I was feeling after my foray into the desert the other day. I came into Togo a few days ago, and was going to spend more time up north because that's where I crossed the border, but Togo has a stupid stupid visa system so I had to come down to Lomé within seven days after entry to apply for an extension, so here I am, in the capital city already. And OF COURSE tomorrow is a national holiday OF COURSE IT IS BECAUSE THAT ALWAYS HAPPENS WHEN IT'S TIME TO APPLY FOR A VISA so I am stuck here until Friday before venturing out to do some more exploring around the country.

Anyway, I had a less than auspicious start to my time here after I crossed the border on Sunday at about four p.m., then had to wait for five hours for the minibus to move from the station even though I only wanted to go a 100 km (all because I think I promised my Dad at some point that I would stop hitchhiking). There was no reason for the minibus to sit there, because all the people were waiting, but it did anyway, because this is Africa and most everything defies logic. So the driver plus about five passengers knew I wanted to get off at Mango and that I wasn't actually familiar with the town, but the bus still managed to blow through the centre without stopping and them dump me unceremoniously at the very outskirts at 11 p.m.

I was over a kilometre away from the hotel, and they were unlit streets. I started walking, and crossed the police barricade at the edge of town. They started to question me as to where I was going, where I was from, etc. Not realizing that the police in Togo are actually NICE POLICE and not like the police in Côte d'Ivoire and Burkina, I adopted a snotty attitude, which was really just a cover because I was on the verge of tears. When they said they wanted to help me, I really did start to cry. Okay, I'm allowed at least one episode like that for each visit to Africa, right?

Anyway, the police eventually ferried me to the hotel on their motorcycle and it wasn't until we were indoors in the light that I realized the policeman was about six foot two and very hunky, so then I cursed myself even more for whole display. He had even said to me on the way over that I must have courage and why was I crying? I didn't think the reply of "I want my pug dog" would wash so I made up some other story about apathy leading to the decline of the country (and it was exactly that profound in my spectacular French, too).

And then, the very next day, as I was sitting under a tree at the side of a river watching the hippopotamus' play in the water, I was thinking, "Oh, how I love Africa!" again. This place makes me schizo!!! The town I stopped in was called Sansanné-Mango, or just Mango for short. It was fitting, I thought, seeing as conservative estimates have put my consumption of that particular fruit at about 60 or 70 since arriving on the dark continent. And I never seem to tire of them. Some days I eat three! What am I going to do when I get home and I have to pay more than 10 cents each for them?

The Togolaise people seem to be a very friendly bunch and in my mind I liken this country to a francophone Ghana. It is small, but very pretty. Lots of lush, mountainous regions, which I greatly prefer to the savannah regions. I'm heading to an area called Kpalimé to do some hiking, which is known for having a lotta lotta butterflies circling your feet as you go. But first I'm going east to Aneho to spend a few days on the beach!!

Hugs, everybody!

Laura xoxo

# Chapter 23
# I Finally Figured It Out!

22 June 2001: Lomé, Togo

Well it has only taken me three months, but I think I've finally gained access into the heads of les personnes Africains!! Life has become oh so much easier since I just started telling everybody that I was married!! I get so much more respect. You see, all along, they just haven't been able to accept the concept of a woman (who is quite obviously over the age of 21) not being married with kids and, heaven forbid, traveling alone. And if I can make a joke out of all the propositions and proposals, so much the better.

Yesterday, I was buying toothpaste from a woman in the market and she asked for my silver Haida-engraved band as a gift. "Why, that's my wedding ring," I said, "that would be a big gift, non?" She just howled (it doesn't take much to make an African person laugh). And the men back off a lot more too, when I say I have a husband, sometimes quite conveniently just in the next village where I will be going to meet him shortly. I also find that getting stern with people here gets you absolutely nowhere. Even when they piss you off to no end, making jokes out of everything gets you a lot farther. Yup, it has only taken me most of my trip to get the culture sorted out, but at least I got there!

I had so much fun yesterday. First, I went through the Grand Marché, or big market. They have these long, beautiful strings of beads for sale which African women wear around their hips, anywhere from two to eight strands, as fertility beads. I decided I wanted to get some just because they're cool, but opted for only two strands as I'm in no maternal hurry.

I picked some out, and then these three hilarious ladies started cutting and joining the strands and measuring them to fit my hips. They completely unabashedly just reefed my shorts down in the middle of the market, totally showing my underwear (and not even my new ones). People were passing by, stopping and laughing at the white chick getting fertility beads. It was so funny. They asked me if I was married so of course I replied yes, to which they gave me fraternal winks and nudges and said how great these beads would be for me. I paid the head shopkeeper lady for them and she gave my bottom a little slap and sent me on my way. And then I was just struttin' down the street, knowing that I had the cool beads on but nobody else knew cuz you wear them under your clothes.

After that I went to the fetish market. Anything dead that you want, its available there!! Togo and Benin are the places where voodoo began, actually, and it was imported to Haiti via the slave trade. But voodoo here had many connotations, good and bad, and is quite an accepted practice, sometimes right alongside Christianity and Islam.

Ooooh, I forgot to mention that the other night when I went to see the live music in Ouaga IT WAS SO GOOD!!! It wasn't a kora player, it was actually one band that had a balaphone player, three drummers, some shaker-thingy people, a flutist, a singer and a dancer. Whew, they cooked. After they played, two of the drummers, a guy and a girl, came and sat at my table with me and we exchanged addresses because they are trying to arrange to come out for the Jazz Festivals in Montreal and Vancouver in 2002. That would be cool. The second group was a four-piece band, and then a whole bunch of different people got up and sang with them. One of the guys was this completely mesmerizing man that had such a deep, resonant voice, very Salif Keita-ish, it was just awesome. So that was the best 90 cent ticket price that I've ever paid, to say the least.

Well, I'm off to Aneho now, after grabbing my passport from immigration first. I'm going to go hop on a motorcycle taxi and hope for the best.

Have a great weekend, everybody!!
Laura xoxo

# Chapter 24
# The Magic of Water

Forty kilometres east of the capital city of Lomé, and just two kilometres from the Benin border is the small and wistfully dilapidated town of Aneho. Once the grand colonial capital of Togo, it now rests quietly on the coastline, stretching out in a narrow strip, checkered with empty lots, buildings that once were grand, and still-occupied dwellings. It is divided into north and south by a lagoon, with one small bridge connecting the two.

After spending several days in the noise and bustle of Lomé, waiting for a visa extension, Aneho seemed the perfect place for me. My time in Africa was winding down, and I felt, with some panic, that I wanted to return to the quaint, small-town lifestyle while I still had the chance. I found it was those settings that provided the richest of my experiences. The cities were great, but time spent there was usually more centred on taking advantage of all the good things to eat, e-mailing, and then eating some more. I'd experience a certain degree of guilt if I were to get hung up in a city for too long, though. It never felt like I was participating in anything of significance, which for me, meant interacting with people. I was much more the passive observer in those circumstances, whereas in smaller places, it was all about getting to know the folks.

Aneho was no exception to this. It was a town that didn't see a lot of action, so people had a lot of time to hang around and talk. When I first arrived, my bush taxi dropping me right in front of a palmy, ocean-front hotel, it was me who was the verbose one. The clerk deposited me in what turned out to be the nicest, cleanest, most-like-a-real-hotel-room room that I'd stayed in since my arrival in West Africa. It had a threadbare little hand towel, soap, toilet paper, and a mirror, and that was just the bathroom! Oh, happy day! Once I'd dropped my bags, I went back out to the front desk to sign in, ecstatic about the room I was about to pay for. I think the clerk believed me to be a mad woman from all the stream-of-consciousness babbling I was doing. Didn't anyone else ever get that excited over a mirror? Sensing that she didn't share in my enthusiasm, I turned on my heel and returned to my room to have a shower with no fear of interruption, and a rarely-enjoyed opportunity to give the old eyebrows a right good plucking.

The hotel had a very pretty, thatch-covered restaurant attached, but it seemed expensive by African standards, and, for some reason, I just wasn't willing to splash out on both the room and the food. I decided to venture across the bridge and down the road, in search of some ladies with some pots with some food. In the dark, they were a bit harder to find, but experience had taught me that if you saw a lady, and then, by the dim light of her candle, you saw a pot, you knew you were in good shape to score some food. I was not in the mood for akoumé (the local version of grits), but some of the pot-women along the way assured me that I'd find someone with rice further along if I kept going, and eventually, I did.

The unfortunate aspect of dining at these road-side benches was that the actual consumption of the meal often took less than five minutes. What was I going to do after that? I had hours stretching ahead of me before it would be anywhere close to bedtime. As it was, I had been retiring at ridiculously early hours in Lomé because it just wasn't all that much fun going out on my own at night only to spend my time fending off the advances of amorous locals. I felt in the mood to linger, but staying there would have been akin to going through the drive-thru at a fast food restaurant and then parking for the evening in one of the stalls just before the exit while you thoughtfully fingered the wrapper on the burger and slowly sipped your cola.

Remembering that I had passed by a small watering hole on my way out, I retraced my steps until I came upon an invitingly-lit room (in the darkness, anything with light was inviting) in the side of a building that was serving as a bar. It had music, and more importantly, two tables set just outside the door, where passing foot traffic could be more readily observed.

One of the other tables was already occupied by three people, and the other had evidence of an occupant in the form of a half-consumed soda sitting on it. I sat there anyway, and ordered an apple soda, my new favourite drink since I'd discovered it in San-sanné-Mango, when the waitress, whose name was Claudine, came out from the bar. It turned out it was her drink that was sitting there, and once she'd brought me mine, she joined me for some conversation. Germaine, who was one of the party sitting at the other table, jumped ship and pulled up a chair with us, and then another fellow happened along a few minutes later, a local school teacher, who took the third and final seat. His name was Iro.

Soon we were all chatting animatedly. It turned out there was a commonality amongst us — we were all married, but with no kids yet! It was getting frighteningly easy for me to tell that fib, and I felt somewhat guilty that our camraderie was largely based upon it. After a couple of sodas, I decided to retire to my hotel room. It was the first time in a long time where I had lodging that actually enticed me to cosy up with a good book and stay in for the night.

The morning came on with an infiltration of clouds that promised precipitation later in the day; even I, with my untrained eye, could see that. Whether its arrival was going to be sooner or later was a greater mystery, but I wasn't about to sit around at my hotel and wait for it to clear. I set out to the north, walking along the main road for a kilometre or so, until I found a dirt path to my right that would take me all the way down to the beachfront.

Traipsing through the long, reedy grass, I came upon an empty, one-room structure that was perched at the top of a slope. From that vantage point, I could watch the goings-on in front of me: a little boy running back and forth with no particular destination in mind, it seemed, and two fishermen that were wading through a shallow, sand-banked part of the lagoon, searching for crabs. I sat down on the concrete slab and stared off into the distance, first trying to obtain some sense of purpose by planning the days ahead of me, and then deciding instead to meditate and reach a relaxed and less-restless state. I couldn't seem to achieve either.

After some time, I realized that the fishermen were yelling at me, and gesturing towards the clouds with their arms. The direction that they were pointing in was more ominously dark grey than the sky that was directly above me, but it still seemed so far off in the distance that I hadn't taken serious notice of it on my own. If anyone knows how to read the cloud patterns, it's these guys, I thought. They wouldn't be shouting like that if they didn't know something big was coming. With a wave of gratitude, I jumped up and turned back down the road from which I'd come. Not even a hundred metres in and literally only a couple of minutes after the start of my retreat, suddenly and dramatically, the skies parted and rain of biblical proportions battered my fleeing frame.

I ran with my head down, thinking I would try and make the few blocks to the main street in the centre of town and take refuge there for a while. Off to my left, I heard the voices of young women, but didn't realize at first that through their laughter, they were calling out to me with the offer of shelter. I passed them, went another dozen metres or so and then, feeling not only soaked to the bone but also strangely disconcerted, I doubled back.

There were two of them, and in the envelope of their arms, they bustled me to cover as familiarly as if I were a girlfriend that they saw every day. One of the women, Joyce, was originally from Ghana and hence spoke to me in English. Angelie compensated for our difference in language with wide, easy smiles. They were at work, and work was a Togolese-rendition of a pub; a room built onto the side of a house, and a small deck. There were three or four tables outside, and a big corrugated metal awning that was decorated with the beer flags of local breweries, but no customers. We talked for a while about nothing, really, and then they resumed what seemed to be their usual places, sitting back in plastic chairs and looking out at the dirt road. We settled into a comfortable silence and I began to wait out the storm.

A few minutes had gone by when a group of children, completely oblivious to our existence, materialized as if out of nowhere and filled the air with singing and hoots and hollers equivalent to what you might hear at a hockey game or on a roller-coaster ride. There were about five of them, all boys, ranging in age from about eight to 10, standing right outside the pub. Down the road, there were also two girls by the next house, about 20 metres away. With no warning, they all stripped down to their bare bones and happy as happy could be, started dancing under the heavy stream of water that flowed from the roofs' downspout pipes.

Their laughter was so contagious that I laughed along with them, although it was obvious that they were having much more fun than I. Probaby having only ever known bucket showers and sponge baths, for them, this was like a waterfall from heaven. They flapped their arms like chickens, using the momentum from their swinging hips to turn themselves around in circles while they bumped and jostled each other for position under the water. This wonderful frivolity went on for at least a dozen minutes, the boys under one pipe, the girls under the other. Being 10-years old and naked in the street was of no concern to them; it was me who was quite astounded by it all, not least by the observation that they were deriving an enormous amount of joy from a very simple thing. It was rainwater pouring from a downspout, something that I wouldn't have even taken notice of. That was it. To them, it was an event.

Eventually, they had all had enough, or maybe their mothers beckoned them back to do chores, I don't know, but they dispersed as quickly as they'd come. There was still no sign of the rain letting up. Joyce, seeing that I was a bit goosebumpy, brought me a sweater to put around my shoulders. She and Angelie then disappeared into the house. I didn't know what had become of them until I went inside and found them curled up on the floor of the bar like two kittens, asleep. It was warmer there than outside, and I didn't really feel like being out on the deck by myself, so I sat down on the floor, propped myself up against a wall with my knees to my chest, and closed my eyes.

Close to an hour must have passed before the pounding noise of the rain hitting the corrugated roof became more of a pitter patter, and the flow from the downspout slowed to a trickle. I was once again restless, and ready to move, but didn't want to wake the women. Instead, I wandered back out to the deck and marveled at the fact that I couldn't have asked for a more enjoyable afternoon. All I had done was sit there. I felt lucky. I, too, had found joy in something very simple.

When Joyce and Angelie rose up and came outside, I grasped their hands in the warm way that Africans do, and thanked them for taking me in. "Will you be back tomorrow?" Joyce asked me, in a way that made me feel like she'd thought it was a nice thing to have me around. I told her that I doubted it, as I would probably be exploring the other end of town. "Have a good time in the Volta region," she said, which was where I was eventually heading to in eastern Ghana, and where she had grown up. "I will," I said, "and I hope that you are able to go back there for a visit soon."

We both meant it.

# Chapter 25
# And It's as Simple as That!

## 2 July 2001: Accra, Ghana

Okay, so I'm riding along in the tro-tro from Hohoe to Akosombo, and the lady sitting next to me pulls a jar out of her purse. It is leaking red chili palm oil or something, and she tries to clean it up with some tissue. I pull a plastic bag out of my backpack and offer it to her. Then she says, "Where are you going?" so I say, Akosombo." So she says, "Aahaauh (pronounced just like that), that's where I live." I say, "Really? Then maybe you could tell me of a guest house, something in the 25 to 30,000 cedi range, because my guide book only lists one hotel there." So she says, "Oh, I can't remember their names, but you will find something." <10 second pause> Then she says, "How long are you staying?" and I say, "One night, then I'm going to Accra." She says, "You can stay with me." So I say, "Really? Okay, thanks!" <Silence for about a minute> Then I say, "What is your name?" She says, "Augusta. What is yours?" I say, "Laura," and she says, "Okay." And that's how easy it is to make a friend in Africa.

Hi everybody! How goes it? I arrived back in Ghana about four nights ago, and I love it!! Again! Ghana is so cool. Even as soon as I crossed the border, I thought, "There are less people picking their teeth with sticks here."

It's a cool place. And I can speak English again, which is a major relief. Two months of French is enough for me, thanks very much. Ach, so much stuff has been happening that I don't even know where to start. Had an interesting episode in Kpalimé, Togo. I checked through my money belt one night, went out hiking the next morning, then went back into my money belt to get some cash for the hotel room and discovered USD $40 missing, yet my room was undisturbed. The hotel manager was pretty damn unsympathetic, insisting that there was only one room key and I had had it with me that day when clearly there was another room key in existence! Or I had a bad case of juju or something.

I saw a couple of Peace Corps volunteers in the town centre and they said that if I went to the police I could just cause more problems for myself, but I couldn't just let it go by without doing something. I took the chance and went to the station, and well freak me green and call me kermit the police were just the most supportive, helpful guys ever!!

They loaded up the van with four guys and we went to the hotel, then they took the manager into the station for questioning not once but twice and held him there for hours until he agreed to pay me back the money as part of his "hotel manager responsibility" for keys and what-not, even though he still insisted he didn't know who the thief was. Anyway to make a long story short, we ended up in front of a magistrate the next morning, and I got 25 bucks back, and a guarantee that he'd change all the locks on the hotel room doors. But the police guys were just so good! I was shocked. I expected them to just shrug their shoulders and say, "too bad, so sad" but they really worked hard for me, and didn't ask for a bribe, either. Very interesting process. So now I've been to court in two countries, and I'm getting better at it all the time. Hahaha!

The Volta region of Ghana was just fantastically gor-geous. I climbed Ghana's highest mountain, which is still rather small, but going straight up in 85% African humid-ity was enough of a strain for me. And coming down was harder — I fell three times! See!! That's why I don't hike! I'm just not the most sure-footed of our species. Much better on skates. Not so good at knowing my own feet. Anyway, I loved the area, and stayed three nights in Hohoe and one night in Akosombo, which is famous for the dam and sits on the edge of Lake Volta, the world's largest manmade lake. And staying in Akosombo with Augusta was really good too. She lives with her Aunty Peace, a big saggy-armed woman who kept laughing at me when I was eating cassava, and her three cousins come for weekends, so they were all there too and it was a lot of fun.

Now I'm in Accra again! I've had enough personal challenges for this trip — trekked in the desert, stayed in the remote villages, climbed a mountain, and now I'm going to the beach on Wednesday!! Chillin.

Some more funny people anecdotes before I go:

I was walking down the street in Hohoe and accidentally bumped a lady. I quickly said sorry as I passed, but she yelled out after me, in that slow, over-annunciated African way, "Why are you beating me like that?"

Dash in Ghana is an informal request for a tip or gift. I usually get asked for dash from people that help me find a cab, or lift my bag off the bus, or stuff like that. The night before that, I was buying fruit from an old, weathered street seller. "Three bananas for 500 cedis," she said. Then she selected what she thought was the best of the lot for me. She handed me four, so I looked at her, puzzled. She gave me a big, gummy grin and said, "I dash you one!"

And after making my purchase from the peanut seller down the block, and him telling me about his younger brother doing military training in Birmingham, Alabama, he called out to me as I was walking away, "Hey! Have a good time in Ghana, okay?"

How could anyone not like this place?

Talk to you soon! From Accra,
Laura xoxo

# Chapter 26
# Fish Ball, Anyone?

Typically, I'm not one to fuss too much about germs and bacteria. I still thaw frozen chicken out on the kitchen counter, I tend to rinse a lot of my dishes rather than wash them, and considering all the weird things I've eaten in strange places, I figure that if I haven't contracted hepatitis yet, it ain't gonna happen. When I saw some of the meat handling practices in the smaller towns and villages along my route, however, it made me shudder. It wasn't troubling enough to push me into being completely vegetarian for those hundred-and-some-odd days, but it had enough of an impact that I still have flashbacks.

With all the information that has surfaced about steroid-fed animals and other strange, yet now common, industry standards, the meat that we buy in North America could be considered rather dubious. Looking pristine on its white styrofoam tray, we continue to eat it, trusting in the 'best before' or 'packaged on' date that is stamped on the packet. Our choice boils down to a matter of perceived freshness, really. The meat that we eat is days, even weeks old by the time it gets to our grill, but it is transported from truck to table by a series of refrigerated receptacles that enable a longer lifespan. So what do you do in Dogon Country, Mali, when it is 42 degrees and you don't have a fridge?

Chickens are easy. You only get one meal out of them, so there's no planning or effort required aside from chasing it down and catching it so you can break its little chicken neck, and then it's into the pot. Cows, on the other hand, can create some concern. There's a lot of beef that comes off those animals, hence the omni-present market meat table: there's the table, and there's the meat, sitting on the table. In a city, you might even see a complete butcher shop in the marketplace. Instead of laying the meat out, the carcasses are hanging, still without the benefit of temperature control. You'd best be holding your breath when you cruise past one of those places.

I learned a few things from my guides while I was in West Africa. For instance, always select your purchase from the vendor that covers the meat up with a plastic sheet or newspaper in between customers, that way, fewer flies can lay eggs on it. That was a handy tip I got from Mamadou one afternoon while we were trekking in Dogon, although I was less pleased once he took the plastic bag of meat cubes he'd bought and shoved it into my backpack to tote around for the balance of the day. It was full four hours before that beef was cooked up for us in the village where we stopped for the night, but I seemed to have survived its consumption.

Transport is another issue. Once you've picked out your slab from the meat table, how do you get it home if you live in another town or village? With many villages only having a once-weekly market, you might have to shop elsewhere if you are cooking for a special occasion.

In one instance, I witnessed some fellows who thought it good enough to just tie their piece of beef onto the roof rack of the minibus and let it hang over the side. I pitied the person that had the window seat on that side of the van and hoped that they weren't wearing their Sunday best, because there was going to be some spattering going on when the driver misjudged the potholes. At least with goats, you could buy them live and carry them on the bus with you to your final destination, but there just ain't no herding a heifer up those three little steps and down the aisle. In Ghana, there were no cows, and hence no raw beef displays. I was told that a certain disease had been running rampant through the country for several years, and it had all but wiped out the cattle population. As a result, the food on the streets was mainly fish, although in some of the nicer restaurants in Accra (the Steers fast food chain or Frankie's in the quasi-ritzy Oku district) hamburgers were still a staple menu item.

There's no point trying to judge quality when shopping for meat in Africa, because basically you get what you get. Whatever the animal, you can bet that it was skinny and malnourished while alive, which translates into stringy and tough once it becomes dinner. As you sit down to your meal, try not to think too hard about the fact that livestock commonly feeds on piles of street rubbish, and deem yourself lucky for just being able to get the meat off the bone. Really, it's not as easy as it sounds.

Practically absent from my daily diet while over there was fresh produce. When I went to one of my first weekly village markets, in Bandiagara, I couldn't figure out what half the things were that were in the vendor's bags and bowls. Eventually, it dawned on me. People have learned to work around the perishables issue just by dehydrating the crap out of everything. You get your vegetables in the form of little compressed balls: tomatoes, onions, okra. I imagine that there is a limit to what kind of vegetables will grow in the soil or sand too, and while imports are available in the city groceries, it is really only the expatriates who can afford to buy them. Even I balked at some of the store prices, instead opting for a steady run of white rice, white pasta, white bread, and couscous, the exotic starch.

There always seemed to be an abundance of people selling dried fish, spread out by the dozens on woven grass trays, their scales flaking off and leaving opalescent specks behind. They were tiny, some with bones, some without, but all types looked highly unsatisfying to me as the main meat part of a meal. You'd have to consume an awful lot to equal the calories from a good salmon steak. I wondered why they didn't just grind the fish up into little balls, too. It could all be like food that you'd take into outer space — get a pot, throw in an onion ball, a fish ball, some water and a Maggi cube and voila! Dinner could be cooked and the liquid consumed in a minute, you know, for those days when they're busy and on the run.

The most elaborate grocery store that I went to in West Africa was in Abidjan. It was in the same plaza that I bought my contact lens solution, and it could have been lifted straight out of Paris or Brussels. I spent a long time walking around in there, picking things up and then putting them back again when I remembered that I had no place to store them, and I couldn't possibly eat everything I selected in just one night. As it was, I sat outside the store afterwards for a bit of escapism and consumed a chunk of cheese, fruit, a croissant, chocolate and yogurt before getting on the bus and heading back to my room, in the heart of the slum. And long live tetra-pak milk (literally), one of my other favourite finds there. I could have cereal for breakfast the next morning! Unfortunately, milk in a box off the shelf didn't taste all that good, but stir in a sachet of Nestle Quik cocoa powder and you're off to the races.

The most fun grocery store that I shopped at was the Booby Market in Bobo-Dioulasso. Just stick your chest out and say that out loud: "I am going to the Booby Market." How could you not have fun? It didn't sell anything that was particularly special and the owner was kind of grumpy, but I still went there twice every day instead of to the other store that was closer to my hotel. I think I still have a plastic bag from there lurking around in my closet somewhere. I should dig it out and take it to work as my lunch bag. It would be my cunning ploy for neutralizing workplace sexism. How taboo can a body part be when the word is plastered all over the place in big, green letters?

Whenever I could, I would sample the special regional or favourite local dish of the place that I was in. Sometimes, it was outstanding. In Sassandra, Côte d'Ivoire, a restaurant owner named Beah created Crab Facil for me. I had to order a day in advance so that the crabs could be purchased at the morning market, but the wait was worth it. Beah scooped all the meat out of the crab shells, mixed it up with yummy things so that it resembled something between a pate and a pasta sauce, and then put it back into the shells for serving. I ate it by dipping my carbohydrate into it (I had a choice of rice or French fries, so I chose fries), and it was superb. Another time, in Ouagadougou, I had Poulet Yassa, grilled chicken served in an onion and lemon sauce. The place that served it up was as hole-in-the-wall as they come, but the food was outstanding, marred only by the Nigerian TV producer that sat down uninvited at my table. He made the same marriage-type proposal that I had already heard so many times before, only this time threw in a cash incentive. I paid the waiter my 85 cents for dinner and left.

Occasionally, I was placed in the position of having to eat or drink something that I thought to be utterly horrid purely out of respect for my hosts. In Santa, Côte d'Ivoire, Mikhael's family introduced me to palm wine. Now, over my years of backpacking on a shoestring, I have become a regular patron of cheap malt and distilled beverages. I don't expect high-quality alcohol when I'm on the road, and if I do come across a decent local brew, then I'm pleasantly surprised. Upon taking my first sip of palm wine, however, my lips tried to disappear down my throat and I damn near stopped breathing. "Lovely!" I said to the seven-odd pairs of expectant eyes around me.

In Akosombo, when I stayed with Augusta and her flabby Aunty Peace, I was invited to join them in the kitchen for a lunch of foufou (fermented cassava, yams or plaintain, cooked then pureed and shaped into, surprise, a ball) and green sauce. The sauce was nothing short of slimy. I watched and waited. "You don't chew it," Augusta said. "Just put it in your mouth and swallow." The first bite went down like jello. On the second bite, I had to count after I put it into my mouth — a-one-and-a-two — then suck it back. By the fourth handful (oh noooo, there were no spoons), my mental count was up to six and I'd had just about enough. I think a fifth bite would have come right back at them in a projectile stream. Aunty, of course, thought this all hilarious, and laughter rippled through her saggy skin in waves. Luckily, after having watched Augusta buy strange seafood items from bus stop vendors on the way down to Akosombo, I had acquired several packets of biscuits and stashed them in my backpack. They came in very handy later on. The tricky part was sneaking into the shared bedroom and stuffing them down without being caught, but I managed to consume enough to keep from going hungry.

There's an element of irony in every story. With regards to my quest for food, it surfaced not when I ate my dinners dished up at roadside tables, nor when my meat was already half-cooked by the sun when I bought it. Rather, irony stared me in the face one night as I puked every hour on the hour and was doubled over from cramps, all after a late afternoon coffee and cake at a chi-chi patisserie. This particular place was owned and run by a French pastry chef, who for some reason had decided to bring European culinary standards to a small town in Côte d'Ivoire. She even had refrigerators.

# Chapter 27
# And It's a Wrap, Folks!

---

## 11 July 2001: Accra, Ghana

It is with some mixed feelings that I write this last e-mail. I am so looking forward to going home and seeing all the family, friends and pug. And I am so overwhelmed that this crazy, glorious three-and-a-half months has come to an end. What a trip it was.

Africa has so many funny little idiosyncrasies that it is even hard to try and remember them in my journal or in e-mail. But from day to day, there are just certain things that make this place what it is.

Colour. People are not afraid of colour. Pink and turquoise houses. Tacky, tacky posters. Men and women in the boldest of bold prints, oddly mixed and matched in a way that will, I'm sure, one day end up in Paris Vogue as being the 'in' thing. Patchwork-painted taxis. Colour is everywhere, and it is big and bright and lively.

---

Sounds. Not a quiet place, this corner of the world. Women in the market can have a raging, screaming feud over a misplaced or borrowed item between them. And it will go on for 30 or 40 minutes! Animals plaintively crying out, goats that look like sheep and sheep that look like goats. The pounding of wooden poles in the grain containers as women work at all hours of the day or night, preparing their staple foods. Laughter, boisterous and loud. And sometimes right in your ear when sitting on a crowded mini-bus. Oh, and music. I will never forget the music. Tinny sounds from small transistors or a thumping, distorted din from the three-foot speakers that people set up outside their shops, playing the same cassette tape over and over again. Does it matter that your shop neighbour across the road also has his speakers blaring? Of course not. And so it becomes a competition, with passers-by suffering the most, and the shopkeepers obviously already half-deaf.

Smells. An area where I am already a little sensitive. Africa has been a full-on nasal assault for me. The gutter stench of urine and rotting fruit and stagnant water. The women who board the mini-buses with a load of fish to transport to the next village. The drifting aroma of beef kebabs on streetside BBQs, which smell fantastic but bring back hideous memories of African 'butcher shops.' The sweet scents of the flowers in the mountains. The acrid odour of a black person's sweat, distinctive from my own.

How plain it will all look when I drive through the streets of Vancouver. No women with enormous piles of anything and everything stacked on their heads. No gatherings of people on streetcorners, animatedly discussing lotteries, or the shortage of rain, or the taxi driver that cheated a passenger. No kids skipping through the streets, pushing a wheel with a stick. No mini-bus ticket-takers speeding past with more of their body on the outside of the vehicle than in, calling out their destination in raspy, shrieking voices — Danquah-DanquahDanquah" or "CircCircCircle." No more quick meals taken from Madame This-or-That at the side of the street, served out of huge, shiny pots in barely-rinsed dishes with hand-made spoons. Nobody offering me brooms or handkerchiefs or Jesus clocks to buy.

It has been good to me, this place. I hope I have been as good to it.

From Accra, five hours before flight time,
Laura xoxo

# Author's Afterword

Almost two years have passed since I sat in the last of what were many poorly-ventilated, rather ripe-smelling Internet cafés with sticky keyboards, hammering away to get my thoughts out in increments of 15 minutes so that I didn't pay extra for the rounding upwards of the elapsed time. As I now read back over what I sent home to my friends and family, I am both glad that I had this method of recording and sharing my travels with them, and sad that it still wasn't even nearly adequate for sharing stories about all the people, all the places and all the things. There was just so much that happened from day to day that didn't or couldn't get mentioned, lest I burn through my micro-budget and end up sleeping on the streets instead of the rooftops!

There were certainly several times in my e-mails where my frustrations with either people or transport (or both) came through quite loudly. I was often using my messages as a means of venting, since I didn't have regular contact with other Westerners that could relate to the angst that some of the cultural differences were causing me.

Personal space (or lack of it) is a good example of one of the sources of my woes in 2001. Coming from Canada, where single-occupant vehicles and large homes with a bedroom for each resident abound, there was a certain difficulty in adjusting to the Here and Now of Africa ("I'll sit here next to you and let's talk right now, okay?"). Whether it was people just being plain, old friendly or vendors being desperately pushy or kids being rightfully curious, sometimes my reaction was that of a person whose space was unlawfully invaded. In Africa, though, the luxury of space and privacy isn't readily available, and hence it is neither contemplated nor observed. I, on the other hand, could not help but to mentally tally how much of my seat space on the bus the breast-feeding women on either side of me were taking up and jut my elbows out like I was a peacock about to strut. The old proverb about choosing your battles was lost on me at the time. I had instead opted for the "Squish, or be squished" approach. I'm sure there were times when I had some poor, unsuspecting (and undeserving of my wrath) African saying, "Geez, I wonder who pissed in her cassava this morning?"

The only times during this trip that I really felt that traveling alone had left me somewhat vulnerable was when I was on the move. Transportation was unreliable, slow, obscure and so completely out of my control that I found it to be the other most difficult adjustment to make. There were certainly times when I wish I'd had someone there to watch my back, or at the very least, my bags.

On one occasion, when I was making the border crossing from Mali to Burkina Faso, I remember that it took me the entire day to move about 200 km within Mali, and, with my fragmented French, I couldn't quite understand what the plan was for actually getting across the border, knowing it was closed between six p.m. and six a.m. Having done the normal bouncing around from truck to truck two or three times, I eventually secured a seat on a vehicle that was moving in the correct general direction, albeit ever so slowly. I didn't dare give it up and seek out an alternative in the form of a room. It was about nine p.m. when we landed at the last town before the Mali border. We pulled over and parked, and I watched and waited. Grass mats were pulled out of the back of the van, handed out, and we all lay down on the side of the road, amidst the hubbub of the hawkers, BBQs, bars, and other border-town commerce, and went to sleep for six hours. Yeah, someone to watch my back would've been nice.

I woke up that next morning all in one piece, to my relief, with my arms still looped through the straps of my backpack and my daypack under my head, substituting for a pillow. There were several other mornings like that, when I would awake and think, "Ah, good. Things appear to be as they should be," even though I had gone to sleep less than certain as to what the night's outcome would be. It is part and parcel of being a Western woman traveling solo in that part of the world, I would say.

While I never felt in danger when I was being propositioned to my face (it was, in fact, usually quite hilarious), once I was in a deep slumber, my personal safety was somewhat compromised. Anything could have happened — the door locks weren't of the best quality, and the windows in my rooms were always open. And, not only did I stand out in a crowd, I frequently realized that everybody else in the neighbourhood or village knew of my comings and goings quite well: when I was at the lorry field waiting for a ride, where I was staying, which restaurants or food stands I preferred. My presence provided economic opportunity; legitimately for the tourist guides and shop owners and local artisans, and not-so-legitimately for those folks who had, shall we say, light fingers. And whether I'd been traveling with a thousand-dollar budget or a ten-thousand dollar budget, it wouldn't have mattered. Whatever the amount of money I had, it was more than they did, and they knew it.

Oddly enough, I used to mentally prepare myself so that, in the event of a robbery, I would be able to say, "Well, I had two-four-six-etc. weeks here, and even though I have to go home now, it was better than nothing." With every week that passed, it was like a milestone successfully achieved — "Still hangin' on to all of my possessions! Yay!" I sometimes gave less thought to who I was actually hanging out with, however, and was a bit security-slack, on occasion, when in the company of men.

Twice on this trip, I slumbered right next to guys whom I'd only known for a day or two (no sex, just sleeping!), and once, I stayed at a house out in the middle of nowhere, with a bedroom door that didn't lock, and the male owner, just down the hall, as the only other occupant. Is this a safe thing to do in Africa? Not particularly. But I did it, I think, because risk is one of those things that I've come to expect and accept when I'm on the road. I've even built up a mental defense mechanism to help me deal with unsavoury situations, should they arise, and survive as a female traveler. It has been a gradual process.

At age 18, in Europe, I was flashed by men three times in three weeks. At 20, I awoke to see a man masturbating into a fellow backpacker's hair as we slept in a train station waiting room in Italy. I've been groped so many times over the years that I couldn't even begin to count. Somehow, I have become very good at separating the physical action from my emotional reaction, and just carrying on. So when an amorous Bobsea stuck his tongue down my throat one evening in Sassandra, or when Mamadou ignored my earlier rebuff of his advances and placed my hand on his manhood while I was sleeping in Dogon, I basically told them to bugger off, but I didn't lose any sleep over it. Sure, I was angry and even did a bit of yelling at Mamadou the next day, but it didn't make me feel afraid or nervous or unsafe.

In retrospect, I could have made better decisions that would have decreased my vulnerability. Perhaps I'm not so much naïve as I am arrogant in my approach, though: because I've been through so much already, I believe there's nothing that I can't handle when I'm on the road. So far, I've not been proven wrong, but some small part of me is starting to wonder if the odds are that my lucky streak might one day run out.

Toward the end of my trip, when I finally wised up and started telling people that I was married, I faced slightly fewer questions about my raison d'etre than before. In general, there were still assumptions made as to why a 30-something-year-old woman, married or not, would be traveling alone through Africa. Unfortunately, from what I heard, there had been incidents involving some of my female European predecessors (slightly older than I) with a penchant for young, supple, black men. I am sure that such events contributed to the perceptions that I ran up against at times.

I'll never forget one such occasion when I was occupying a bar stool at one of the local hangouts (okay, so maybe that didn't help matters either). I got into a great discussion with the bartender there over what the definition of a woman's purpose in life was. By his account, it was to bear children, plain and simple. When I told him that I would likely never have any kids myself, his eyes flashed angrily and he demanded, "But what, what are you going to do with yourself then?" My answer of career, travel, relationship with partner, it was all lost on him. I almost thought he was going to deny me service from that point on because of my admission.

As a starting point for finding accommodations in West Africa, my guidebook was my saviour (I carried one of the popular budget mainstays, written by the same folks who now have a TV show to match). It named places and people with rooms to rent that I would not have otherwise found. It warned of places which were noisy brothels (in general, brothels were fine, as long as they were quiet), which places had toilets from hell and were next door to discos, and which places had no fans. I could then plan ahead and look forward to my nights of misery! It was to be expected, though, traveling on the budget that I was.

The option of rooftop sleeping turned out to be a godsend in the heat of Mali, and though it took hours of traipsing through the sandy desert roads of 45-degree Dori (Burkina Faso), fully loaded with all of my gear, an oasis of air-conditioning was eventually found right where the guidebook said it would be. The key to finding a decent place to crash was being able to just roll with things.

Once, en route to Mopti, I had met up with two other travelers on the overnight bus. When we arrived in town in the morning, we were escorted to a private family home where, for a fee, we could use a room in the house to store our gear, and sleep on the roof at night (the use of private homes is apparently quite frowned upon by local officials). Quite satisfied with that arrangement, we went to sleep at about 10 p.m. after having been out to enjoy a beer and watch a spectacular sunset over the River Niger. About an hour into my sleep, I awoke to look around the rooftop and find that about seven other people, family members, had joined us. How silly of me it was to assume that we were getting private use of the facility! But, hey, not a problem! (The problem actually turned out to be the next day, when we practically had to wrestle them to get a half-bucket of water to use for a sponge bath. Water was sparse in those parts, that was for sure).

Now, back home, there are times when something will occur that will prompt my recollection of a story or event, and I'll share it, in all its glory, with whoever is around at the time — friends, colleagues, and less often, my family (they might sometimes get a bit freaked-out by my adventures, I'm afraid). Often the response I get back is something along the lines of "Wow, that sure doesn't sound like fun to me," or "I know I couldn't do that. Why do you put yourself through that?" The short answer is that, for me, for a fairly significant amount of pain, there is an immeasurable gain or reward. When the going is tough, it is really, unimaginably tough. Then, just when you think that you've most definitely arrived in hell a few years early, something will happen that will be so unexpectedly cool or unique that all the anguish that led up to getting there dissipates within seconds (until the next day, anyway, when the cycle begins anew).

Is this kind of traveling for everyone? Most definitely not, and I wouldn't attempt to sell anybody on trying it out if it hasn't already made it onto their list of "Life Things To Do" via divine inspiration, inherent curiosity, or other means. These kinds of trips are on the lowest end of the budget-travel scale. This time around, I took just a backpack and always paid for rooms, whereas on previous trips, my tent and sleeping mat road atop my pack and often saved me a dollar or two along the way. They can also be more stressful than fun unless the trekker is able, consciously or not, to look past the risks that are inherent to traveling in the developing world. Vaccinations provide a percentage of protection from a standard list of diseases and viruses, but there are still lots of other ailments that can cause great discomfort and malaise, as well as innumerable challenges that are par for the course.

For me, however, trips such as these provide so many experiences, so much knowledge, and such great opportunity to see people and things and culture that is so different from my own (yet still so fundamentally human), that the benefits far, far outweigh the risks. I would do this again in a heartbeat. I loved the places that I went to in 2001, and if the chance arose to visit them again, I would. There are yet other places in Africa that beckon me — Morocco, Algeria, Tunisia, Libya, Ethiopia, as well as more countries in West Africa, and other areas in Central Africa. And then there is the rest of the world... Burma, Suriname, Iraq, the Stans. Ah! The list is endless.

The one small regret that I have, (it is the same regret that I always have after a trip), is that I did not take more photographs. Perhaps I am the type of person that best experiences things face-to-face, rather than through the eye of the lens. I'm not sure. I feel, though, that I have neither the quick reflexes required to capture a fleeting image, nor the patience required to seek out or wait for an optimal image of something or someone. Hence, I try to record and describe what I saw through my writing. The uncensored (and also unedited) e-mails that are included here are of the real day-to-day trials and self-indulgent musings of a solo traveller on the road. By adding the stories, I have tried to continue with some of the themes that I first pondered in my personal journals, also adding some of the stories that I didn't have time to construct in the cafés.

Admittedly, the initial idea to share my stories in book format was not my own. Now that I've joined in on this collaborative project, however, it has become all the more important to me that my audience feels some of the same things that I felt and sees some of the same things that I saw. I'm not saying this because I feel that I have some great insight into the dynamics and complexities of these cultures. Sometimes I didn't even fully comprehend what I saw. It is not even that West Africa as a region in particular must be experienced and understood. It is because all parts of this globe should be given equal consideration and attention, all people on this planet seen as we see ourselves. We must respect one another, and our differences, and realize that there are many more similarities. This is where the path to peace begins.

Laura Enridge
June, 2003

# Glossary of Adinkra Symbols

Throughout Ghana, I noticed the incorporation of what I thought were absolutely great shapes and patterns on clothing, in woodwork and on other mediums. I was overjoyed when I received an entire set of stamps of these symbols as a gift last year. I chose my favourites, based on their meanings, to use throughout this book. Below, they are matched up with their descriptions.

The beautiful symbols for which Ghanaian art and culture have become known actually derive their name from Ivoirian royalty. King Adinkra was an early nineteenth century figure in the Ivory Coast who allegedly made a replica of the sacred Ghanaian Golden Stool. The stool, carved with bold symbols and patterns, was considered sacred and served as a throne for Ashanti royalty. In return for his disrespect, the King was allegedly captured and beheaded by the Ashanti people. Later, the symbols that had adorned his garments and been on the stool were adopted by local artisans and incorporated into everyday use.

## Adinkra Symbols

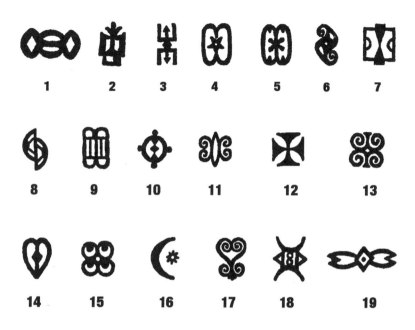

1. Truth
2. Enjoy Yourself
3. Understanding
4. Hope
5. Goodbye
6. I Shall Meet You Again
7. House of Peace
8. You Have Changed
9. Two Good Friends
10. Faith

11. Forgiveness
12. Good Fortune
13. Strength
14. Have Courage
15. Wisdom & Knowledge
16. Faithfulness
17. Learn From Your Mistakes
18. Good Living
19. Peace

# Things to Pack

- A good travel pack: you don't have to spend large dollars on a high-end backpack to find something that will serve you well, but don't cheap out on the department store special, either. Pick one that has good, heavy zippers, a sturdy internal frame, and lots of pockets. Get an employee from the store that you buy it from to shape the frame to fit your form. Take something that holds at least 50 litres. I prefer the jumbo 70 litre size. As for toploading or full zipper, I travel with only the latter, whereas Europeans tend to like the former. A toploading pack is more streamlined and graceful, but if you want something from the bottom, it all has to come out. A full zipper pack is wider and bulkier (I have taken out many an innocent bystander with mine) but is much easier to organize and access.

- Sleeping bag or cotton sleep sheet, either is good as long as it unzips: you'll want to be able to stick your feet out.

- Micro fleece: wear it on the plane, then use it as a pillowcase the rest of the time. Easy to wash out and it dries in minutes.

- Music: it will be one of your only connections with home.

- Antihistamines: especially if you have dust allergies. You'll see plenty of dust. Pills are available, but are expensive at the pharmacies.

- Contact solution: Hello, take a bazillion bottles and sell them to other travellers!

- Two pairs of socks maximum: you'll never use them.

- Camp towels or cotton sarongs: both are good because they dry quickly after you've showered, and are way easier to wash than regular towels.

- Cotton sports bras: Leave the Victoria's Secret stuff at home. It will get wrecked, and the nylon will just give you heat rash anyway. Same goes for underwear.

- Convertible trousers: take at least two pairs of the nifty zip-off-at-the-knee pants. They are rugged, easy to wash and dry, and take up very little space in your backpack. Don't even bother taking jeans or heavy twill stuff if you've got these.

- Lotsa tank tops, a couple of t-shirts: you'll want to be as minimally clothed as possible, so sleeveless is better. Expect to go through two a day, and do not, really, do not bring white!

- One long-sleeved shirt: there may be places where you want to be able to cover up from the sun, or to go in a mosque, or whatever.

- Good shoes: invest in well made, cushioned walking sandals and shoes. I'll never forget when I hiked through east and southern Africa in my Converse All Stars and was having to ice my bruised heels every other day by the time I got to Zimbabwe.

- Bathing suit: something cheap so you won't care if you forget it on a clothesline somewhere along the way.

- Feminine protection: if you buy imported stuff while abroad, it will be expensive, and if you buy locally made, it will be akin to cotton wool.

- Sunscreen and mosquito repellent: take just a bottle of each of the stuff you like; you'll find it easily enough on the road and you'll go through it like there's no tomorrow.

- Minimalist first aid kit: it's good to have a few of the essentials, but most of the basic stuff can be purchased in Africa, and for much cheaper. I always pick up a few needles and syringes when I get over there so that if I ever need an injection, I can supply my own gear.

- Guide book: I once travelled from Kenya to South Africa without a guide book, but in West Africa, I don't know what I would have done without it. Make sure you pick a book with good maps!

- French dictionary or phrase book: The language came back to me quickly in part because I would study these at night.

- Water bottle: lots of places sell their cheapest water in little plastic bags, which you can then pour into your plastic bottle.

- Things you can trade or give away: little flag pins, stickers, crests, and pens are absolutely loved by the locals and will make you a big hit. Don't give them to people who seem to expect such gifts, though. Give them to people who you think will be genuinely surprised and delighted.

- Money belt: absolutely essential.

- Cash: unfortunately, cashing travellers cheques can be a royal pain in the ass in West Africa, so in addition to your cheques, take a healthy chunk of cash with you (and guard it with your life). Save it for the times when you can't cash cheques, or for when the commissions are almost as much as the amount you are intending to change. As for currency, take either U.S. dollars or Euros. You don't need to purchase any local monies ahead of time; you will have no problem finding Joe Blow on the sidewalk outside the airport to make your first exchange with. Occasionally, you may also have luck with a bank machine that will accept your debit or credit card. Mine never worked, but I found a couple of places where I could process Visa cash advances inside the bank.

- Flashlight: for all those outdoor showers in the pitch black.

- Camera protection: the camera I took was très heavy, but all the buttons and lenses were specially sealed to protect it from water and sand. If your camera isn't, make sure you have a good case to protect it from such ingress.

- Swiss Army knife: you don't need the heavy, deluxe version, just the simple knife and can/bottle opener model will do.

# Things Not to Pack

- Nightclothes: you're better off sleeping in one of your regular pairs of shorts and t-shirts when you're in a shared accommodation, and when you're alone you'll be naked because it's so damn hot!

- Short shorts: Wearing these is like saying, "Ogle me."

- Too many basic toiletries: you can easily and cheaply get toothpaste and soap. If you only like to use salon shampoo and conditioner, then bring it, because that you won't find. I suggest a spray leave-in conditioner, because this will help protect your hair from the sun.

- Cosmetics: believe me, you won't be wanting to put foundation and other gunk on your skin. You'll sweat it off in two minutes. Truthfully, I did bring just eyeliner, mascara and a lipstick, because I do have my girly-girl moments, even on the road.

- Hairdryer: let go of the idea that you will ever have any kind of reasonable hairstyle whilst on a trip like this. Do bring hair ties and clips, because you'll always want it tied back and off your neck during the day.

- Mosquito coils: they'll just disintegrate into pieces on the way over, and they're cheap and easy to find everywhere in Africa.

- Anything really expensive or that you really love: prepare yourself for the fact that the risk of theft is high on any road trip, anywhere, and don't take anything that you would be heartbroken to lose.

Laura Enridge is a tech sector planner and coordinator by trade, but a writer at heart. Every so often, she leaves the comfort and safety of that predictable world of business for areas not so commercial and conventional. During her time away, to the delight of her friends, she writes. She has traveled extensively in Europe, the Middle East, Australia, Latin America and Africa. Previously, Laura has had her human-interest and travel stories printed in local newsletters and newspapers. She lives in Burnaby, British Columbia with her pug, Ozwald.